DISSIPATION
BOOK ONE

Yorkshire Publishing
TULSA

ISBN: 978-1-960810-71-7
Dissipation

Copyright © 2024 by R.O. Carol
All rights reserved.

No part of this publication may be reproduced, distributed, or transmitted in any form or by any means, including photocopying, recording, or other electronic or mechanical methods, without the prior written permission of the publisher, except in the case of brief quotations embodied in critical reviews and certain other noncommercial uses permitted by copyright law.

Cover image by Freepik.

For permission requests, write to the publisher at the address below.

Yorkshire Publishing
1425 E 41st Pl
Tulsa, OK 74105
www.YorkshirePublishing.com
918.394.2665

Published in the USA

R.O. CAROL

DISSIPATION

To my husband Cody, for being an unwavering source of support, and to my friend Kelly, for if it hadn't been for your encouragement, this book would still be an unfinished draft.

1. MORA
DECEMBER 2072

Mora had lost count of the number of days she'd been at Ascensio's in-patient residential facility. She tried to recall how many days ago it was that she'd sat facing Dr. Pine in an office that had become all too familiar. As usual, she had been silently observing her psychiatrist without really seeing her. The woman's mouth moved, but the words drifted past her, until one particular phrase had caught her attention for the first time.

"There's a new drug being tested," Dr. Pine had told her. "I think you would be a good candidate for this drug, should you wish to partake in the study. It is your choice, of course . . . and I must warn you, there could be side effects."

Hearing this, Mora had looked at Dr. Pine—for the first time, really looked at her. The doctor wore her dark brown hair back in a simple but elegant bun. Her face was clear of any blemish. She wasn't strikingly beautiful, but she was pretty. Her features seemed perfectly symmetrical. She wore a white pantsuit tailored exactly to her figure. Mora couldn't spy a single piece of lint on it, and she suddenly felt envious of the sheer togetherness that the psychiatrist represented—however sterile she might be. Mora felt that she was looking at her antonym incarnate.

"Do you think it will fix me?" Mora had finally replied, exhausted.

"My job is not to fix people," Dr. Pine chided, then offered a soft smile, "But, I think it could really help you."

So, they had scheduled Mora to receive this miracle drug that would keep her from falling completely over the edge.

"Mora?"

Mora blinked and found herself back in the present moment. Normally, her psychiatrist saw her in an office a few floors down, but today was different. She sat in an exam room that was immaculately clean, devoid of any colors other than white, gray, and the palest blue.

"Uh, sorry, what were you saying?" she asked Dr. Pine.

"I just need your signature here, and we will begin your treatment." Dr. Pine slid Mora a pen and a clipboard with a bunch of paperwork Mora had no intention of reading.

When she had finished signing, Mora was instructed to lay back on the cushioned exam table.

"Some patients feel a little dizzy after the treatment," Dr. Pine explained.

Mora lay still as Dr. Pine cleaned her arm with an alcohol swab and then took a syringe full of clear liquid from a silver exam tray.

"Best to look at the ceiling and count to three," Dr. Pine encouraged.

Mora took a breath and looked up at the ceiling just as everything went black.

2. ALETHIA
NOVEMBER 2072

Alethia stirred in the early hours of the morning. She was anxious for her first day. It had been her dream for several years to be hired on at Ascensio, Inc: *a restorative institute finding solutions for the betterment of the human condition.*

She'd studied clinical psychology at Perrington University and finished her program with honors just two months ago. She felt primed, confident, and a bundle of nerves all at once. Accepting that she would not fall back asleep even though it was only just after three in the morning, she rocked herself up into a seated position and got out of bed.

After pulling on a pair of leggings and a sports bra, she crossed over to the other side of her flat and climbed

DISSIPATION

on the treadmill. With earbuds blasting and shoes laced just a bit too tight, she willed herself to run.

Alethia lived a fast-paced, busy life. She often felt that she carried the entire moon on her back as the earth spun beneath her. Running was one of the few things that eased her internal tensions.

Shower, coffee, makeup, blouse and slacks pressed just so, she paced back and forth through the flat until she had triple-checked she had everything she would need, and off she went to Ascensio, Inc.

The long, private drive to the gate was meticulously groomed, not a single blade of grass out of place. Orb-shaped shrubs and tall palm trees were spaced evenly. Yellow and pink flowers were dotted around harmoniously. The black asphalt gleamed in the early morning sun of a cloudless day.

The towering spherical infrastructure was blinding as it reflected the sunlight. Several other buildings snaked around the giant sphere, which reminded Alethia of an egg in a nest. Ascensio, Inc. appeared to be made entirely of black glass that masked what lay inside. The complex sat on the outskirts of Desert View, the city in District 8 that Alethia called home.

A slim woman in a business suit and glossy lipstick greeted her from the security window at the entrance gate. Her white teeth expressed a cordial smile as her eyes peered down with scrutiny.

"Good morning. Do you have identification?" she asked.

"Of course!" Alethia fumbled through her bag until she grasped the plastic-encased badge she had received from a high-security drone just the day before. The woman scanned the badge.

"Welcome, Alethia Burkshire. Orientation will take place in Wing Seven. Take the second exit on the roundabout and follow the signs for parking from there." The woman handed Alethia a parking stub that read:

11/22/2072 07:20. Security Clearance Level 1.

Alethia thanked the woman and proceeded as the gate opened for her. She was relieved that she had arrived so early, as it took her nearly twenty minutes to locate the designated Seventh Wing parking garage through the maze of roundabouts and driveways.

DISSIPATION

Alethia had never been inside the gates before. The complex was enormous, just as manicured and gleaming up close as it had been from afar. The desert sun rising over the distant mountains warmed her face as she closed her eyes and exhaled. *Here we go.*

Once she found her way to the check-in desk in Wing Seven, Alethia got in line behind the other new employees signing in.

"Please follow the signs marked for orientation. You will begin your training in the auditorium down the hall to the right," the woman said in a monotone voice.

Down the hall and to the right. Relax, Alethia told herself.

3. ODEZA
NOVEMBER 2072

Odeza flicked his right wrist up to check the time and continued walking down the long corridor towards Wing Seven. He would get there just on time if he kept this pace. However, he felt the annoying pain of a hangover in the back of his eyes and made a sudden veer into one of the employee breakrooms.

He poured a generous amount of sugar into his cup of coffee before rummaging through the cupboards for some aspirin.

Odeza caught a glimpse of himself in the mirror that hung on the wall of the break room, and he instantly regretted his decision that morning to skip shaving. Black scruff was making an appearance, as were bags underneath his grey eyes. His black hair was a tousled mess, as usual. He haphazardly straightened his tie and suit jacket before chugging his coffee.

"Well, well, well, what do we have here?" Elizabeth Straumen, Odeza's primary superior, leaned against the doorframe wearing a tight grey pencil skirt, matching blazer, and red pumps. She crossed her arms, which pushed up her already-showing cleavage and twisted her mouth into a lipstick smirk.

"Good morning, Liz," Odeza replied with the corners of his mouth turned up slightly as he stirred his coffee.

"Isn't there somewhere you're supposed to be?" she asked, lifting one perfectly waxed eyebrow.

Odeza took a sip of his coffee and looked up at her from the rim of his cup.

"I wouldn't dream of being anywhere else," he replied, sauntering past her through the doorway. She did not move to the side to make room. She turned her head over her shoulder to watch him leave.

The auditorium of Wing Seven was packed with eager, anxious new faces chattering softly. Odeza navigated the crowd with ease, gliding onto the stage. The din of the room softened to a dull buzz before fizzling out completely.

"Good morning, prospective new hires," he began, his voice deep and purposeful. His eyes scanned each face, row by row, as he spoke. "Now that we've completed check-ins, we will begin orientation. If you have not already, please find a seat. Don't worry, you won't be sitting for *too long*." He flashed a grin.

Odeza paused for a moment as everyone settled in and continued to scan the crowd.

"You have made it through a rigorous and cutthroat recruiting process to get to this point! For that, you should feel proud. However, you are far from securing the position you applied for—whichever position that might be." At these last words, he waved his hand to the side.

The room stirred, and murmurs of concern began to rise.

"Now, now," he chided into the microphone. "To be selected for this corporation is an honorary achievement, and the worthiest among you will get your rightful place." Odeza paused for a moment to let this information sink in, then continued softly, "You will be given ample opportunity to showcase your abilities to the selection committee."

The prospective employees turned towards each other to chatter with puzzled looks on their faces. This part of orientation was Odeza's least favorite part. He already had a headache, which made it even more irritating when the noise in the room began to rise again. It was always the same nervous, antsy energy at first. He was eager to get the groups to move on to what would be more fun—at least for him.

"Okay, okay, settle down," he scolded, tapping the mic. "I will make short work of the rest of the opening. My name is Odeza Speer. I am Ascensio's Orientation Leader. I have been with Ascensio for ten years now. It is my pleasure to welcome you all and begin orientation.

"We'll now divide the fifty of you into five groups of ten. Each group will enter a separate training room where its members will compete in a set of challenges. The best of the best of you will, of course, win the five open spots," he said, knowing this was all completely new information to them. He rushed to finish his last sentence before the noise of the room had a chance to rise. "If any of you do not wish to move forward, please exit the way you came at this time. My assistant, Angie, will now break you up into groups and give you further instructions."

With that, he was off the stage and out of the auditorium in a few long strides.

4. MORA
AUGUST 2072

Mora awoke in her stuffy and insufferably hot bedroom. She covered her eyes with her hands to shield them from the sunlight streaming through the window. She figured it was probably noon. Her mouth was parched, and the ache in her head seemed to pulse. She had a flashback of the night before.

She had gone to dinner with her boyfriend, Jaxon. He'd seemed distant again, wearing that faraway expression that always made her want to scream.

She'd ordered a glass of wine with her dinner to help her relax. When she caught him eyeing her warily, it had sent her over the edge. "What?" she had hissed, bating him.

"I thought you were taking a break for a while," he had said in a tone he used with her more and more lately. It always made her feel as small as an ant.

"I can't have a glass of wine at dinner without you making me feel guilty? Nice, Jax. Really supportive. I am trying, you know. I am trying to be better."

"How can I be supportive of you when you never do the things you say you're going to do?" His voice had risen slightly, attracting sideways glances from the neighboring table.

There it was again—that ball of knots in her stomach that she could only soothe by drinking herself into oblivion. She was not good enough and would never be good enough. She followed her routine of shoving all feelings into a wadded-up ball and stuffing it down deep into the chest of secrets that was inside her.

"I want to go home." Her voice was faint and colorless.

They didn't speak for the entire drive. After Jaxon left her apartment, Mora opened a new bottle of wine from her stash and did not stop drinking until she was numb.

5. ALETHIA
NOVEMBER 2072

Alethia found herself among a shuffle of chaos in a corridor off the auditorium's south-facing wall. Her assigned group was told they were going to go to the "Orientation Arena". While she did not doubt this facility was big enough to have an arena, she grappled to figure out what part of orientation would *warrant* an arena.

Her mind swirled, trying to predict what kind of competitions she would be faced with. While this already did not seem like what she signed up for, she was too far in to even consider quitting now.

Outside a massive black door, the assistant, Angie, had each group of ten lined up one after the other. Four more employees entered one by one from an adjoining hallway, each of them taking a position in front of a different group.

"Group One, please follow Andre," Angie instructed, gesturing towards the black door. Once Group One had gone through the door, Group Two followed suit, and so on, until it came time for Alethia's group, Group Five.

The big black door led into a long and very tall corridor that curved around, the end out of sight. Their group leader stopped outside of a door on their left.

"Please enter and wait for further instructions," she said.

One by one, the group of ten silently followed each other through the doorway. No one was bold enough to question the leaders directly in case it jeopardized their chances at one of the coveted positions.

"First, let me formally introduce myself," the group leader said. "My name is Piper."

Piper grinned, her blackish eyes twinkling. She was short and petite, with cropped red hair and freckles. She wore a green polo shirt and grey slacks that narrowed at her ankles and rested just above her black street shoes.

"I have worked at Ascensio for somewhere around eight years now," she continued, "and I've worked in the orientation department for the last two. I'm sure you're all a bit nervous and thrown off by our induction process—trust me, it was the same for me. But I encourage you to just go with the flow and trust the process. I can assure you that everything we do here, we do for a reason.

"Our group's first challenge will be a maze. Once we descend these steps, you will take your starting places, and when you hear the buzzer go off on the big countdown clock, it is fair game to begin. Remember: You are up against fifty other competitors in the long run, not just this group of ten."

Piper let this information settle for a moment as she made eye contact with each of their stoic faces. She then turned on her heels and marched towards the steps that descended into darkness. They all followed.

One by one, the orientees were escorted off the small landing at the bottom of the stairs and into narrow, black corridors that seemed to make a circle around what Alethia could only guess was the arena.

She was left alone facing yet another black door. If Alethia didn't have anxiety flooding her limbic system before, she certainly did now.

An icy voice echoed through the halls from an intercom. "Ladies and Gentlemen of our new-hire selection pool, this will be your first challenge to compete for one of our open spots. When the door in front of you opens, you must enter the maze and be the first to get to the center. You will have fifteen minutes. When the clock runs out, if there is not a proper winner, the person closest to the center will move on to the next task."

The door swung open. Alethia squinted as her eyes slowly adjusted to the somehow even darker space in front of her. The walls and floor were sleek and black, with small white orbs spaced out ahead, just bright enough to see the outline of the walls. The ceiling high above appeared to be tinted glass, no doubt where they were being watched from. A huge timeclock was sprawled across it, already counting down the seconds. The sight of this pushed her forward, the pressure suddenly boiling up inside her.

However, as she took her first step, she froze, eyes darting to the floor. Where she stepped, there appeared a neon-purple illumination of her footprint. She took two more steps, and two more glowing purple footprints appeared.

DISSIPATION

Alethia realized that, should anyone cross her path, they would be able to follow her right to the center. This frustrated her, but she had no time to waste—nearly an entire minute had already passed.

Cautiously, Alethia picked up her pace. She paused at the first junction, uncertain whether to turn right or left. Glancing over her shoulder, Alethia examined the illuminated markings of her steps. The footprints closer to the door were fading quickly, the first few already invisible. *There must be significance to that*, she thought. *Why track our prints, only to have them disappear?*

Scanning her surroundings once again, she spotted a blue diamond, barely visible above the juncture. Underneath appeared a simple algebraic equation: $3L-24=21$.

Alethia frowned at the symbols, her mind racing. She had never exactly been great with numbers—the best she could manage, especially in her stressed state, was that 21 plus 24 was 45, so 3L equaled 45.

What was 45 divided by 3? She thought.

She started counting by threes on her fingers ... 15. L was 15.

"But what am I supposed to do with that?" Alethia wondered aloud. By now, all of her footprints had faded, aside from the two directly beneath her. She looked to her right, then to her left, then at the clock overhead. The time remaining was 12:42. At a loss, she chose the path to her left, once again leaving a trail of glowing footprints behind her.

She came to another juncture, and immediately checked the space above. Sure enough, there was a symbol and an equation. This time, it was a circle, and the accompanying equation proved similar to the last: 2R+12=62.

Okay, simple enough, she thought, *62 minus 12 is 50, 50 divided by 2 is 25. R is 25. But what does it mean?*

Eleven minutes remained on the clock.

She tried to keep the numbers in her head. *L is 15, and R is 25.* She knew these must be clues of some kind—was there a puzzle ahead that would require her to remember the number sequences?

She took another left. This brought her to a new juncture, only this time, there was no symbol or equation up above. Alethia hesitated but decided to go right. She walked for a while before coming to a dead end.

DISSIPATION

Her heart began to race. She ran back, following the quickly fading trail of footprints. By the time she reached the last remaining one, she was out of breath and in a panic. For a terrifying, fleeting second, she thought it was all over, that she was hopelessly lost—only to glance upward and discover that she was standing beneath that familiar circle, its equation taunting her: 2R+12=62.

She took a deep breath.

"Right, okay," she breathed out. "L is 15, R is 25."

Suddenly, it hit her.

L. R.

Left. Right.

Could the equations be telling her which way she should go?

R is 25.

She glanced at the clock overhead; time was running out. There was no choice but to follow her hunch. Taking the path to the right this time, she counted her steps until 25 footprints glowed behind her. To her great relief, she looked up to find another symbol and equation. She beamed and glanced up at the clock. It read 9:32.

The third symbol was a triangle over the equation 4L-15=45. She calculated that 45 plus 15 is 60. *Does 4 go evenly into 60?* She crossed her arms and leaned against the wall, trying to crunch the numbers. As her shoulder made contact, its surface emitted that familiar purple glow.

Of course! She jumped back and used her finger to write the division problem on the wall and quickly came to the answer: *Again, L is 15.*

She took 15 paces to her left and spotted another diamond. Recalling the diamond from before, she hoped L would again mean 15. Gaining confidence, she picked up her pace. She prayed that she had finally figured out the formula—but even still, there was no telling how far she was from the center, or how far along the others were.

A shrill ding from above signaled there only was one minute remaining. Panicking, Alethia hurled herself around a corner—

And collided with one of her competitors. Sprawling onto the dark floor, they gaped at each other for half a second. Then—before either could react—an impressive display of dazzling lights exploded from the end of a corridor that had, until then, been shrouded in shadow.

After wandering for so long in the darkness, Alethia was momentarily blinded. Once her eyes adjusted, she saw a pedestal with a red buzzer.

Amazingly, she'd found her way to the center of the maze.

Alethia was the first to move. Her exhaustion evaporated as adrenaline shot through her. She was on her feet before she even knew it, sprinting toward the button as if her life depended on it—and, for her, it did. She heard a groan from behind, followed by rapid footsteps pounding the dark floor. He was gaining on her. She could almost feel his breath on her neck. But as panic threatened to overtake her, she suddenly remembered—

This is what you've been training for.

She pictured herself on her treadmill, the pounding bass from her headphones compelling her to take one more step—and then another—and another—

Alethia threw herself toward the buzzer and smacked it as she collapsed onto the floor, gasping for air.

6. ALETHIA
NOVEMBER 2072

There were no congratulations, no acknowledgements. Before Alethia could even catch her breath, Piper was there, ushering her to the next challenge. Alethia struggled to keep up as they made their way through the winding, dark hallways.

Piper stopped abruptly in front of a black door that was indistinguishable from all the others lining the walls of the corridor.

"Your next challenge is beyond this door," Piper said.

"What about the rest of my group?" Alethia panted. "Will they be sent home?"

Piper eyed her condescendingly. "A word of advice, my dear ... if you want to succeed at Ascensio, you should learn to focus on the task at hand. As I was saying, your second challenge lies behind this door. Unfortunately—assuming you do complete it—I won't be there to escort you to the third; the following challenge will begin immediately."

Alethia searched Piper's face for any indication of what was coming, but the woman's expression was unreadable.

"Here, you'll need this," Piper said impatiently, thrusting a necklace into Alethia's hands. "Good luck."

The door opened, seemingly of its own accord, and Alethia stepped into an impossibly dark chamber. The door swung shut behind her with a force that told her there was no going back.

Gradually, she found that the darkness wasn't all-encompassing. At the far end of the room, a lone spotlight was suspended from the ceiling in front of a tall glass tank. Under its faint light, she could just make out a massive closed floor drain beyond its open doors. As she cautiously approached, a dull, buzzing sound drew her attention to a green neon sign above the doors, spelling out a single word: *Enter.*

Alethia's stomach clenched in fear. *You have got to be joking,* she thought. Despite everything in her telling her not to, she entered the tank. The second her feet passed the threshold, the glass doors slid shut, sealing her inside.

Panic gripped her. She banged on the glass and threw herself against the door, desperate to break through. Eventually, though, she had to accept that it wasn't going to crack. She fell backwards against the wall and slid to the floor, staring defiantly into the space outside the tank. But there was nothing to see—only darkness.

She turned her attention to the interior of the strange trap. Her gaze passed over the large drain at the center, the tile floor, and a lever attached to a pipe that seemed to lead out of the tank. Her eyes tried to follow the pipe into the darkness.

Just then, a second spotlight blinked on above an identical tank about twenty feet away. Inside the tank were the nine other orientees she had competed against in the maze challenge. The looks on their faces were full of the same fear and shock that hers must have been. All their eyes were fixed on Alethia.

DISSIPATION

An exposed pipe in her opponents' tank burst open, and water began spilling into the space. Some of them screamed. They were all trying to find a way to scale up the side of the sealed tank, but it was impossible.

Alethia watched as they squirmed about, the water up to their knees already. They banged on the glass and yelled obscenities at the orientation leaders, who were nowhere to be seen.

Alethia's eyes returned to the pipe in her tank controlled by the lever and followed it again. Her eyes had adjusted enough to see that her pipe connected with the tank of her opponents.

She was filled with dread as a realization came to her. If she turned the lever, the water from the other tank would empty, saving her opponents, and filling her tank.

She knew this was a challenge and assumed they were testing her ethics: Would she save herself or save the lives of nine others? *Surely, they couldn't be in real danger of drowning, right?* She asked herself. Either way, she knew what the right thing to do was.

She placed both hands firmly on the lever and pulled it to the right. As she had predicted, water from her opponents' tank began flooding out of their tank and into hers.

The other orientees looked around at each other with relief and then at Alethia. When the water from their tank was empty, the double doors opened and they all rushed out, not desiring to relive their experience. They exited the room, and she was alone.

The water was up to her waist. With the others gone, Alethia figured it would be safe to switch the lever back. She pulled on the lever, and it closed off the gushing water. She sighed in relief.

Another pipe on the opposite end, one Alethia had not noticed before, began spewing water into her tank. She felt a surge of panic. *What is going on?* She wondered. *Did I make the wrong decision? Did they want me to demonstrate self-preservation above the protection of others?* The water was creeping up her rib cage. There was no other lever.

Panic rose in Alethia's chest; every particle of her body was imploding with a sense of urgency to escape the tank. Goosebumps covered her body as the water inched towards her chest. She looked down at the necklace with the red button that Piper had given to her. She had forgotten all about it. She pressed firmly, praying that it might help her.

The same calm and icy female voice from the maze resounded in the room: "Remain calm. Help is on the way."

The water did not stop flowing into her tank. She pressed the button again, and the same exact message echoed in the room.

Alethia was absolutely puzzled. The water was now sloshing around her neck. She was freezing. She felt along the sides of the glass for something she might be able to climb. There was nothing.

Was she supposed to solve a puzzle, like in the maze? Her eyes darted frantically around for some kind of clue.

She willed herself not to cry as she felt the water closing in. She recalled the echoing voice... *Remain calm. Help is on the way*. Did she dare trust that?

Alethia now had no choice but to try to tread water to keep herself up, as the water would surpass her head otherwise. She looked up at the spotlight and squinted. The top of the tank was a good twenty feet up, but she couldn't make out what it looked like because of the blinding spotlight.

Alethia continued treading water, waiting. *Remain calm. Help is on the way.* All she had now was her mind; there was nothing her body could do but tread the water. She forced herself to not let anxiety overtake her. *Remain calm*, she said to herself. She closed her eyes and flattened herself into a back float.

She could hear the water sloshing around the perimeter of the tank. Her hands, well wrinkled by now, moved rhythmically through the cold water. She counted silently in her mind as she focused on keeping herself afloat.

Minutes ticked by. There was no one coming. The tank continued to fill, and Alethia continued to rise. Floating on her back, she had to keep her eyes closed so the light above wouldn't blind her. She could see fireworks behind her eyelids. Floating bursts of orange, yellow, then deep blue and purple.

I can breathe, she reminded herself, *I'm okay*.

Suddenly, Alethia heard a different sound among the constant sloshing. She could hear water hitting the ground. She had reached the top of the tank. There was no glass enclosing her. She resumed treading water and looked around, blinking away the dancing orbs the spotlight left in her vision. She could see around the rim, her head above the top of the tank now.

How am I going to get myself down? She wondered. Should she crawl over the edge, she would drop at least twenty-five feet onto a concrete floor. She continued searching. She could look past the spotlight now that she was at the top. Her eyes strained. Then she smiled. There was the outline of ladder rungs above her to the far right. She paddled over and grabbed hold.

The moment she took hold of the bottom rung, the drain at the bottom of the tank opened. The water surged down and left her hanging by one hand onto the rung as the tank emptied at an impossible vacuum-like speed.

She had no choice but to pull herself onto the ladder. It was either that or let go—likely breaking her legs and remaining trapped in the tank. She firmly grasped the bottom rung with both hands and used every bit of strength she had left—which wasn't much. She'd been treading water and floating for so long that her body was weak. Her hands were slippery, but, driven by adrenaline, she did what she might have thought impossible in a different circumstance; she pulled herself up, using only her upper body strength, until her feet were in reach of the rungs, and she climbed onto a landing.

A few feet away, Piper emerged from the shadows to greet Alethia.

"Well done," she said, arms crossed, sporting a smile that Alethia could only describe as wickedly amused.

7. MORA
OCTOBER 2072

It had been sixteen days since Mora had anything to drink. It filled her with pride and hope that she could, in fact, be the person that she wanted to be. She and Jaxon had hardly fought at all since she had started seeing Dr. Pine.

She recognized that she had put herself and Jaxon through hell the last two years. But, for the first time in a long time, things were looking up.

She had started going to the gym daily, and the results were noticeable. She stepped on the scale to find that her weight had dropped eight pounds. She smiled with satisfaction at the scale and stepped off to face her mirror.

Her smile faltered as she lifted her shirt to examine her stomach. She pinched at her side. While she was far from being overweight, all she could see were areas she wanted to improve.

* * * *

Jaxon and Mora met at the park. They laced their fingers together as they walked under the autumn leaves.

He smiled down at her.

"I'm really proud of you," he said, stopping to cup her face in his hands and kiss her. The warmth in his smile had returned, yet Mora could still feel him fall into reservation at times. She figured things would take time to go back to normal, and she couldn't blame him. She just felt grateful he had not abandoned her. God knew she had given him plenty of reason to.

She returned his smile and hugged him tight, as if she could keep him with her like this forever.

After a minute, he chuckled and pulled away, lacing their fingers back together as they returned to their walk.

"Hey, want something to eat?" Jaxon asked. "I'm starving,"

"Oh shoot, I ate before I came," Mora lied. "But I'll happily watch you eat," she said with a sideways grin.

8. ODEZA
NOVEMBER 2072

"Oez, are you quite finished stuffing your face? We're ready for you to start your next interview," Elizabeth, again with her arms crossed, chided Odeza.

He leaned back in his chair and tipped the potato chip bag he was holding to his mouth to finish off the crumbs.

"Coming," he mumbled, food in his mouth.

They left the break room and Elizabeth filled Odeza in on his next orientee.

"She's through with the maze and the tank," she said, flipping through her binder of profiles. "Alethia Burkshire. She did well in the maze, but so did her runner up, Max Martin; she barely beat him by seconds. It was rather entertaining. And she lasted in the tank for the whole challenge."

"Okay. Anything else I should know?" He paused outside of the door to the room where Alethia would have to face him for questioning. It would be her next challenge.

Elizabeth pressed the binder of profiles into his chest and snarked, "Well, she's pretty, so you'll probably enjoy that."

And off she went. Odeza rolled his eyes. Elizabeth made no secret of her . . . *fondness* for Odeza. He played along with her flirtations. She was his supervisor, and it benefited him to do so despite having no interest in her.

She could be a pain when she wanted to be, so he kept himself on her good side. However, it irritated Odeza when she got jealous of other women she felt threatened by.

Odeza ran his fingers through his tousled black hair and made sure he had no potato chip crumbs on him before pushing open the door to his interrogation room.

The room contained a large, blocky, black desk with a chair on either side, one for him and one for the orientee. The room had green walls, the color of a maple leaf in summertime. There was a one-way mirror on the left side wall where the review board was no doubt already situated and watching.

Odeza adjusted his black tie and sat down as he thumbed through the binder for his assignment with Ms. Alethia Burkshire. The review board had already done enough research on each orientee to come up with lines of questioning that he would perform.

The maze had been Alethia's *mind* challenge. How quickly could she use her brain to get herself through a time sensitive situation with little information? The tank was first designed to test her ethics; would she save nine others or herself? Then, she'd been given a follow-up test in the tank of pure willpower and the ability to remain calm in crisis. *This* challenge would determine how she would hold up against uncomfortable pressure and a scrutinous line of questioning. Odeza delighted in the task.

The intercom buzzed. "Are you ready for her, Mr. Speer?"

"Send her in," he replied.

The green door facing Odeza opened, and Piper ushered her in, silently gesturing for her to sit.

Alethia Burkshire was indeed a sight. Her features were mostly meek: she had a small nose and a delicate chin, but stern eyebrows sat above golden-brown eyes that looked directly at him, unwavering. Her petite frame gave reference to toned muscles as she moved. Her honey-blonde, long hair was still wet from the tank, moving around her in tangles. She had been given a dry set of plain, tan, scrub-like cotton pants and a matching shirt.

She sat, nodded once at him, and quietly said, "Hello," before looking down at her clasped hands.

"Ms. Burkshire." Odeza extended a hand for her to shake across the table. "I hear you performed well in your first two challenges."

Alethia quickly shook his hand and looked up at him.

"Is this the part where you tell me what the point of all that was?" There was leashed anger in her voice, her face carefully neutral.

"What point do you believe it had?"

"Well, to figure out whether I'm worthy to work here, I assume. But the *method*—"

"And are you? Worthy to work here?"

Alethia fumbled. She sat back in her seat and narrowed her eyes at Odeza.

"Is this another challenge?"

"You didn't answer my question." Odeza's features were schooled. He held her eye contact, watching her bite her lip as she considered.

"I think I am worthy to be here, yes," she finally mumbled, looking away from him.

"Am I supposed to believe that?" Odeza challenged, lifting an eyebrow. He expected her to play into his bait and answer defensively, but instead, she straightened in her seat.

He watched emotion drain from her face before she looked back up at him and said, "I have a degree . . . I graduated with honors. I have come through all the challenges so far. I—"

"So, you're qualified," Odeza interrupted. He knew he was being watched and was expected to continue trying to derail her, yet he found himself having to focus harder than usual. It was typically easy for him to unnerve people.

Alethia stared at him. He could see hurt in her eyes. He didn't doubt she was not used to being spoken to this way, which was part of the point.

"I care about helping people," Alethia finally responded.

"Lots of people do," Odeza countered. "I would hope all our applicants felt that way. What makes you *worthier* than them?"

"Nothing," Alethia responded. This time, she didn't look down after answering. "I'm not more worthy than anyone. Worthiness is a subjective qualifier. I can consider myself worthy or not worthy, and someone else might have a completely different opinion. But I want to work here. I'm qualified to work here. You can figure out for yourself whether I'm *worthy* enough. I can't convince you that I'm good enough." An unidentifiable emotion flickered on Alethia's face at her last two words.

Odeza didn't have a chance to respond before the intercom buzzed, notifying them that time was up.

At the sound of the beep, Alethia dropped her intense eye contact, and her posture seemed to slump. She suddenly looked worried. Odeza made note of these changes as he stood. He wished to make eye contact with her again, but she wouldn't meet his gaze. She stood and Odeza walked her to the door and opened it for her, gesturing with his right hand for her to enter the hallway where Piper was waiting. Alethia quickly exited.

* * * *

Later that afternoon, Odeza found himself fixated on a singular carpet square in his office as he ran through what had been one of his worst interrogations. He kept replaying their conversation in his mind.

Odeza's office door opened abruptly, snapping him out of his reverie. Elizabeth appeared to be in a particularly hostile mood as she dropped a file folder on his desk.

"The selection committee has reached a verdict. You'll be happy to know Ms. Burkshire made the cut." With that, she sauntered out of his office.

9. MORA
NOVEMBER 2072

The phone conversation that Mora just had with Jaxon was not good. He was temporarily moving six hours away to Fort Kenzington for an assignment. He had called to let her know he'd be leaving tomorrow. As if ripping off a band aid. He had said he'd been waiting to tell her until he'd made his final decision. He had told her that she'd been doing *so well* lately, and he felt like she could handle him being gone for a while.

After they hung up, Mora threw her phone across the couch she was sitting on in her desolate apartment. She stared out the window, feeling an icy numbness creeping through her. Jaxon would be six hours away. She was all alone.

Mora idly picked at the seam in her jeans as she sat staring out the window. She thought briefly that it was odd that she wasn't crying.

She could have been sitting there for hours for all she knew. All she could feel was a gaping void slowly gnawing her core.

She wanted to cry. Wanted to scream. Yet nothing came out.

His words prodded at that gaping hole inside her. *She'd been doing so well. She could handle it.* Why was everything so wrapped up in what she could or could not handle?

Quite frankly, Mora felt like she couldn't handle a goddamn thing these days. Every engagement, every obligation, every commitment sent her mind spinning into dread.

Mora had spent so much time mourning the life she always wanted. She had imagined so many things for her life, had so many goals and ambitions when she was younger. Yet she caused her own downfall every day. She was the wrecker of her own dreams because she could not get better.

DISSIPATION

She wished she knew what was wrong with her and why she couldn't just *be* better.

10. ALETHIA
DECEMBER 2072

A week ago, Alethia had received an e-letter from a high-security drone from Ascensio, Inc. offering her a position as an "intake specialist."

Since leaving Ascensio the day of her orientation challenges, Alethia had thought a lot about her experience. She still felt baffled by all of it. After her awkward interrogation with the prick of an orientation leader, Odeza Speer, she had been very casually debriefed by Piper, who explained that the challenges were uniquely designed to test for elements critical to the success of any new hire. Piper then informed her she should expect to hear about their determination soon; and with that, Alethia was unceremoniously dismissed.

DISSIPATION

When Alethia learned she had been offered a position, her first feeling was one of accomplishment and excitement. She had accomplished her goal. But that feeling was soon replaced with apprehension. Given what she had experienced with orientation, what would it be like to actually work there? But Alethia knew she couldn't pass on the opportunity. She had to at least give it a shot.

So, she had accepted the offer. Her first few days consisted of very standard paperwork and training videos on confidentiality and workplace expectations.

Today would be her first day of onsite training. Her stomach churned at the thought of the email she had received about her schedule for the day: she was supposed to report to the office of Odeza Speer at eight o'clock to start her first day of training.

She had not seen Odeza since his cold and painfully uncomfortable interview with her during the challenges. She pictured him: How his grey eyes, like daggers, pierced into hers. How he'd towered over her with those broad shoulders. His face would have been almost angelic, anatomically speaking, had it not been twisted into an expression of cold judgment.

Alethia tried to suppress the rising feeling of nausea as she zipped her jacket and headed to work.

* * * *

Alethia arrived early, as she always did. It was 7:42 when she checked her watch in the empty hallway that led to Odeza's office. Her footsteps echoed as she approached the heavy oak door. The frosted glass that framed it was dark.

Alethia took a seat in one of the two leather waiting chairs outside the office. She crossed her arms and lightly tapped her fingers against her elbows. Not long after, she heard footsteps echoing down the hall. Her heartbeat quickened. *Please, don't be . . .*

It was. His figure and gait were unmistakable. She tried to find something interesting to inspect on the hem of her shirt. She could tell his eyes were on her as he approached. She glanced up to acknowledge him, trying not to be awkward.

A shadow of black scruff outlined his mouth and cheeks. His black hair looked freshly showered and combed back. He wore black dress pants, a white button-up shirt, black tie, and a black jacket. A leather computer bag draped from his right shoulder. He walked unhurriedly. His face looked drawn, tired.

"Good morning," Odeza said. There was no hostility in his tone. It was neutral, cordial even.

She had expected him to chastise her for being so early.

"Morning," Alethia mumbled. She could smell his cologne as he unlocked his office door inches from her.

Once he entered, Alethia didn't know whether to follow him in or wait outside until it was eight. Professionally, she wanted to display politeness. Personally, she wanted to give him the cold shoulder. She could hear him turning on his computer and shuffling papers on his desk.

"Ms. Burkshire." Odeza's words were a clear invitation to enter his office.

Alethia slowly stood up and turned to face the doorway.

He gestured with an open palm at the chairs facing his desk. She crossed the threshold and did not meet his eyes until she was seated. She cleared her throat and prayed for courage.

Odeza did not speak right away. He seemed to take his time examining her face. Finally, he spoke.

"How are things going so far?"

"Everything's great," she replied automatically, trying her best to make her voice sound confident and unbothered.

Amusement flickered on Odeza's face; his dark steel eyes penetrated her. *Don't back down*, she told herself. She willed herself to smile at him.

"I get the feeling I didn't leave you with a very good impression of me," Odeza said with a hint of sarcasm as he leaned back in his chair.

"Is that what you meant to do?" She fired back, and then mentally scolded herself.

Odeza paused, the amusement intensifying on his face.

"Well, no, not exactly," he finally said, "That wasn't my prerogative . . . circumstantially speaking."

"Aha, and what exactly was? While we're on it, what was the point of that conversation? What was the point of soaking me in a tank full of water?" She could feel her cheeks getting hot, embarrassed for expressing emotion in front of him.

"Everything we do here—" Odeza began.

"I know, I know, it serves a purpose," Alethia finished for him.

"Something like that," Odeza replied.

"So, who are you really?"

"I'll let you continue to be the judge of that."

She stared at him. He stared back. Neither of them spoke for several seconds.

"You are going to get a tour of the facilities today," Odeza said, suddenly all business. "You've been assigned a clinical supervisor, Dr. James, who will walk you through more of your job-specific duties. After the tour, you will spend the remainder of the day with him."

"Okay," Alethia said with a nod.

"This Friday evening, Ascensio is hosting a mixer at the Regal Suites on Broadmoor Street that will serve as the company's holiday party as well as an opportunity for new hires and everyone else to get to know each other outside of work. It's optional, of course, but everyone is welcomed and encouraged to attend," Odeza explained.

Alethia's eyes went wide. The Regal Suites had to be one of the most expensive venues in the city to host a company party. And there had to be hundreds of employees who worked for Ascensio, at that. Alethia could feel the social anxiety of meeting and interacting with so many new co-workers rising in the pit of her gut. *And what will I wear?* She thought.

"Alethia?" Odeza interrupted her thoughts and she realized she had not replied to him.

"Sorry—um, I'll be there," Alethia responded habitually and realized in that moment that she should not have committed herself so hastily. *Damn.*

"Excellent. Well, shall we?"

"Shall we what?"

"Start the tour," Odeza said slowly, raising an eyebrow.

Embarrassment once more flooded Alethia. She mentally scolded herself for making herself look like an idiot, again. She nodded once and stood from her chair. Odeza swiveled in his chair slightly away from her to stand, not quite hiding a bemused smirk.

* * * *

Alethia's tour ended up being rather short, considering the massive size of Ascensio, Inc. She was, of course, not shown *everything*, just the parts of the facility she was authorized to work in. She was shown a large office space with cubicles, where she had been assigned one in which to complete her daily reports and paperwork after intakes. There was a conference room for meetings with a large solid oak table and plush leather chairs around it, as well as a break room furnished with lavish amenities like an espresso maker and fancy black leather couches. Then there was the adjoining hallway of offices where the clinical supervisors were housed.

Finally, she was shown her unit for intakes. The unit reminded Alethia of every standard doctor's office she had been in when she was little. The waiting room had magazines and a little water cooler. The intake rooms themselves had exam tables for the doctors if any patients that came in needed medical attention. There were heart rate and blood pressure monitors. There was a small desk with a chair on either side, where Alethia would sit with the patient to perform their intake.

The intake unit did not open until nine, so there had been no one around while Alethia had toured it. Odeza brought her back to the hallway where the clinical supervisors had their offices. He stopped in front of a door with a name plate that read Patrick James, PhD, LSW. Odeza knocked.

A surprisingly young and handsome man with a broad smile opened the office door.

"You must be Alethia," he said warmly with an outstretched hand.

Alethia reached to shake his hand. Before she could reply, Odeza cut in, "She's all yours, doc." And off he went.

11. ALETHIA
DECEMBER 2072

Dr. James ushered Alethia into his office. Behind his desk were floor-to-ceiling windows overlooking the desert plain and distant mountains that surrounded Ascensio. The rest of his office was rather ordinary. There was a sturdy wooden desk with an expensive-looking computer resting atop. He had a plush, black office chair and two matching chairs sitting across from his desk. To the left of his desk, a solitary wall hanging depicted a rugged mountain landscape.

Dr. James plopped down in his chair. He had short, light brown hair that was slightly longer and tousled at the top. He was dressed in khaki pants and a pale blue, checkered, button-up shirt, the sleeves of which were rolled up to his elbows. His eyes were emerald green. He was clean-shaven and had immaculately white, straight teeth. Alethia noted his muscular build and relaxed posture. She estimated he was probably in his early thirties.

"Well, now that we're rid of *that* stick in the mud," Dr. James mused, "sit, sit, please. Would you like anything to drink? I can have Amalia bring us some coffee if you like?"

"Sorry—Amalia? I haven't met her yet," Alethia said as she sat facing Dr. James.

"Oh, of course! Amalia's our office secretary. She's a doll, you'll love her." With that, Dr. James picked up his office phone and paged her. "Amalia, I want you to come meet our new intake specialist. Would you be an absolute dear and bring us some espresso? Thanks, hon." He hung up and turned back to Alethia.

"That's very kind of you, thanks," Alethia said.

"Well, I'm sure you got no hospitality from Odeza Speer. Really, I promise you, we aren't *all* cranky Suits here," Dr. James chuckled.

Alethia felt herself relax in her chair and smiled a little, pleasantly surprised by Dr. James' candor.

"I will admit I am happy I'll be reporting to you, Dr. James, rather than him," Alethia confessed.

"Patrick, call me Patrick," he replied with a charming grin that faded to a frown as he continued. "I'm afraid you *will* still report to Odeza for orientation purposes." Leaning forward, he whispered, "He's got his hand in a lot of pots here."

"Ah . . . " Alethia replied, not quite sure what to make of that.

"But don't you worry," Patrick said with a wink. "We like to have lots of fun here."

There was a soft tap on the door before a stunning and petite blonde woman let herself in, carrying a tray with espresso, cream, and sugar.

"Amalia! Perfect timing. This is Alethia Burkshire. Alethia, meet Amalia," Patrick said, gesturing back and forth between them. "Thank you so much for the coffee, dear."

Amalia set the tray on his desk and smiled down at Alethia. "It's a pleasure to meet you." Her smooth voice sounded like honey.

"Likewise," Alethia replied, smiling back as she shook Amalia's manicured hand.

"If you ever need anything, I'm in the corner office past the conference room," Amalia said and gave them both a nod as she gracefully exited the office.

"Well, I suppose we should get right to your training," Patrick said, smiling around the rim of his espresso mug.

* * * *

Alethia spent the next several hours shadowing Patrick as he performed intakes. Each one took roughly thirty minutes. The patients all seemed somewhat delirious, many of them manic or suffering from hallucinations.

Alethia had learned about each and every psychological disorder that had been categorized in the *Manual of Disorders of the Modern Age.* It had been something of a bible to her during grad school. However, she found that no amount of studying had prepared her to confront the reality of human suffering in the flesh. She felt emotionally exhausted by the third intake of the day.

She watched Patrick with admiration as he spoke gently to the patients, showing endless compassion and patience. He had told Alethia several times that she was doing an excellent job staying composed through some of the outbursts. One of the patients had screamed obscenities at them.

"Alright, there is just one more today that we have scheduled at three. How are you feeling?" Patrick asked with genuine concern in his eyes.

"I'm good," Alethia tried to say convincingly with a soft smile. "Just a little tired, that's all."

"The first day is always the hardest. It gets easier, I promise," Patrick reassured her. "How do you feel about taking the lead on this last one? I'll be right there to help if you get stuck."

"Oh . . . " Alethia faltered.

"Trust me," he said, placing his hands on either of her shoulders. "You're a natural. I can tell."

Alethia blushed and smiled back. "Alright then, let's do it."

* * * *

Back in the intake room, Alethia sat across from a thin young woman with unbrushed brown hair and red-rimmed brown eyes. She was slumped in her chair, her face solemn.

"Hi, Mora, it's nice to meet you. I'm Alethia."

Mora looked up at Alethia, her face unimpressed. She said nothing.

"We're going to go ahead and get started with your intake, okay?"

When Alethia again did not get a reply, she went on.

"It says on your record here that you've been in to see Dr. Pine. Do you consent to continue seeing her during your stay here?"

A shallow nod was Mora's only response.

"Excellent. As all our patients in this unit are self-admitted, do you agree to receive treatment here and stay for the duration recommended by your doctors?"

Another nod.

"According to Dr. Pine's notes, you've been struggling with some depression and anxiety, along with alcohol abuse, and, more recently, disordered eating. Do you find that to be accurate?"

Mora met her eyes. Alethia noticed tears welling up.

"Yes," she said quietly as a single tear slid down her cheek.

DISSIPATION

Alethia felt moved with compassion for this young woman and reached for her hand.

"We're going to do everything we can to help you, Mora," Alethia said firmly.

She meant every word.

12. ODEZA
DECEMBER 2072

The Regal Suites on Broadmoor. It never failed to disappoint. After tipping his taxi driver, Odeza sauntered into the magnificent hotel. The ceiling of the lobby had to be fifty feet high, with glistening chandeliers that reflected on the wall of glass elevators. The polished stone floor gleamed. Groups of small pine trees aglow with white lights were clustered throughout. People dressed in their finest moseyed around him.

Odeza knew the way. Ascensio often had its holiday party at the Regal, and they always reserved the grand ballroom. He made his way past people who were talking excitedly with their significant others or families.

The holidays always gnawed at Odeza. While it was the most wonderful time of the year for some, it was a pretty damn lonely time for him. Odeza knew that if he wanted marriage and a family, he could have it. But while Odeza had met and dated many beautiful women, he had never met a woman he was interested in enough to want to spend forever with—let alone produce offspring with. His cynical view of marriage and family always prompted him to keep his relationships brief.

And these damn holiday work parties. He hated them. It was the same every year. Over-the-top decadence to boast of the company's success. If people weren't getting drunk out of their minds and making fools of themselves on the company's dime, they were sucking up to their superiors. Their superiors, in turn, would strut about like peacocks, boasting about their own great successes in life. Odeza usually kept to the bar, which is where he was headed now.

The grand ballroom, as expected, was decorated handsomely, with Christmas trees everywhere. Long buffet tables laden with steaming food lined the far wall. Tables for sitting and eating were strewn about and topped with pinecones, holly, and white candles. So many white candles. There was a dance floor in the center and a bar on the right side of the giant space.

Odeza had purposefully shown up late, and the ballroom was already packed. At the bar, he ordered an Old Fashioned. Drink in hand, he leaned against the far end of the bar to survey the crowd.

He spotted Elizabeth. She was already trashed. She threw her head back and cackled as she placed her hand on the shoulder of one of the executives she was talking with. Odeza smirked to himself. So typical.

His eyes continued to lazily watch his fellow employees, as if he were at a spectator sport, until they snagged on Dr. James. He was talking to a woman in a sparkling silver gown that touched the floor, her honey blonde hair curled and pinned up. The woman was facing away from Odeza.

He admired the shape of her figure. Patrick was no doubt being an obnoxious cad. Odeza watched his over-animated face contorting into stupid expressions as he told some story that probably wasn't true to the woman. She leaned forward and placed her hand above her chest as she laughed, turning slightly as she did. Odeza nearly choked on his whiskey as he saw the profile of her face.

It was Alethia Burkshire. The only new hire to ever trip Odeza up on his orientation interview. The only one to challenge him. The audacious little thing. Odeza quickly looked away. He ordered another drink to stifle whatever emotion was forming in his chest and took a seat at one of the bar stools. His plan tonight was to avoid as much conversation as possible, stay just long enough to be noticed by his bosses as having made an appearance, and go the hell home.

"Can I get a glass of Riesling, please?" That soft, but certainly not weak voice made Odeza's back go stiff. *Shit.*

He turned to his right, and there she was.

"Oh," Alethia said, surprise written on her face, "I didn't recognize you sitting over here. Hi, uh, Mr. Speer."

"Odeza," he interjected as he took her in. She was wearing more makeup tonight than he had ever seen her in. Not that she needed it, but the red lips and winged eyeliner made it hard to look away.

"Right. Got it," she said and turned back to the counter.

"Are you enjoying your evening?" he tried, wanting to engage her just a bit longer. Then he would leave.

"Yeah," she gushed, letting a rare smile towards him fall to her lips. "This place is insane. I've never worked for a company so loaded."

Despite himself, Odeza chuckled. "Yeah, that's the impression that these parties give, isn't it?" He smiled and took a drink from his glass.

"Why are you sitting over here by yourself?" She asked him.

"I don't like to socialize," Odeza replied candidly, though he felt some heat rise to his cheeks at the observation.

"Then why come?" She countered, "You said attendance wasn't mandatory, didn't you?"

Odeza was at a loss for words. He took in her face again. She was utterly unfazed by him.

"You like it then?" Odeza deflected. "The socializing."

She looked to the side and pressed her lips together.

"Well, no, I guess not really. I was terrified to come. But I'm glad I did," she confessed.

"*Terrified?*" He raised an eyebrow at her.

Alethia rolled her eyes. The bartender handed her the glass of white wine she had ordered.

"But you're glad you came," Odeza pressed.

"Yeah, it's been pretty fun—"

"There you are! Gosh, I was beginning to think you'd gone home," Patrick exclaimed as he squeezed past the people standing and talking near the bar.

Patrick came within inches of Alethia before stopping and placing a hand on her shoulder. Something about that enraged Odeza as he stared at Patrick's hand.

"I just got my drink, chill out," she replied with a smile, lightly pushing his shoulder. "And I ran into Odeza here." She gestured to Odeza.

As if he had not seen Odeza prior to that moment, Patrick animatedly slapped an expression of surprise on his face and said, "Oh! Hey there, buddy! Didn't see you there." Patrick lifted his hand from Alethia's shoulder and extended it to shake Odeza's in greeting.

Odeza stared at that hand, waiting until it had settled back to Patrick's side before replying flatly, "Patrick. Always a pleasure."

"You're not here all by yourself tonight, are you Dezzy?" Patrick said, his voice full of disingenuous concern.

Odeza leaned back in his chair and crossed one leg over a knee as he chugged the remainder of his drink.

"You know me, Pat, all I need is a few rounds of drinks. Chases the loneliness right out of my lonely soul. What about you? Got a date tonight?" Odeza asked pointedly.

"Nope, not tonight, buddy. Just got the marvelous company of our newest and greatest *ever* intake specialist," he cheesed, beaming down at Alethia, who blushed and looked away.

"Well, that is just *lovely*," Odeza drawled, watching their faces. "I will leave you both to it, then. Have a great evening." Odeza set his whiskey glass on the bar, unhurriedly got up from his seat, and walked out of the party, forcing himself not to look back.

13. ALETHIA
JANUARY 2073

Patrick had been right. The more intakes Alethia did, the easier they got. She had been working at Ascensio for a month now, and she still deeply empathized with the various new patients who were so clearly struggling, but she found herself falling into a rhythm. She would come to work early to prep her intake sheets for the day, do two to three intakes, eat a lunch she packed from home in the break room, do a couple more intakes in the afternoon, and then complete all the paperwork and data entry in her cubical before leaving for the day.

Alethia felt best when she was good at whatever it was that she did, and her confidence grew as she became comfortable in her new job.

She had begun to make friends with her co-workers. On a few occasions, she had gone out to lunch with Amalia, and she felt very comfortable with her supervisor, Patrick. He never failed to brighten her day when she had difficult intakes.

It had been weeks since the company party, and she hadn't seen Odeza since that brief exchange. She had received a few emails from him with paperwork for her to fill out but nothing else.

If there was anyone she had met at Ascensio who seemed even a little disagreeable, it was Odeza. She could not seem to get a good read on him. Each encounter she'd had with him had been strained in some way or other.

Alethia glanced to the bottom righthand corner of her computer screen to check the time. 4:45. She was finished with her paperwork for the day and more than ready to head into the weekend.

"Hey, you!" Patrick chimed, rounding the corner of her cubicle. He casually leaned on her desk. "Good work today, great stuff. Got any big weekend plans?"

Alethia straightened the stack of papers on her desk as she replied, "No, not really. What about you?"

"Well, I was actually wondering if you wanted to go to a hockey game. A bunch of us are going, and I have an extra ticket. It's yours if you want it."

Alethia paused, a little unsure of what to make of the offer. She had not spent time with Patrick outside of work before. Before she could respond, another figure was at her cubicle.

"I'm afraid she'll have to miss the hockey game this time," Odeza said with his hands in his pockets. He looked at both of them but offered no other greeting.

Patrick's face heated, and he spoke in a tone Alethia had yet to hear come out of him. "Why is that Odeza?"

"Because she'll be with me."

Alethia nearly choked. She looked at Odeza incredulously.

"I see you haven't checked your email," Odeza said, examining his fingernails.

It was true. Alethia hadn't checked her email for the last hour or so. She began clicking away to find out what *exactly* Odeza was talking about.

"I'll save you the time," Odeza sighed. "Ascensio has decided to send you on a business trip to tour some of our other facilities and provide feedback from your perspective of the quality of them. They're calling it '*case-study surveying*.'" Odeza slid his hands back into his pockets and looked down at the other two with a bored expression.

"I heard nothing about this," Patrick objected, crossing his arms.

"I take it you haven't checked your email either?"

"Well, not recently. I—"

"It's all there, Patty, I promise. I took the liberty of assigning the workload Alethia will miss to two of your other subordinates." Odeza shifted his eyes to Alethia. She held his steel gaze unflinchingly for what was likely only seconds but felt like minutes. "I'll pick you up in the morning at six. Our flight is at ten."

With that, Odeza sauntered away before Alethia could even respond.

Patrick didn't so much as look at Alethia before storming out of her cubicle, muttering something she couldn't understand.

* * * *

DISSIPATION

Alethia got home to her flat and immediately started a hot bubble bath. She helped herself to a large glass of wine and slid into the tub. Massaging her temples, Alethia replayed, for the seventy-seventh time, what Odeza had sprung on her.

A business trip? With him? After scrambling to read through the email he had sent, she learned that she and Odeza were to fly to three different districts over a week's time. A *week!* Alethia hadn't the slightest clue how she was going to survive an entire week alone with him. There had to be some way she could get out of it. Alethia found herself feeling as she had with the orientation challenges—like someone was messing with her.

But she knew that she couldn't make a fuss about going. It would look like a slap in the face to turn down their *gracious offer* to go sightseeing for a week and get paid for it. She also knew that there was really no way to explain why she *wouldn't* jump at the opportunity.

Alethia took a long drink from her glass of wine and sank deeper into the tub. The bubbles and steam swirled as she sighed. She could do it. It was only a week. She could survive one week of *sightseeing*, Odeza be damned.

* * * *

As he said he would be, Odeza arrived outside of Alethia's flat at exactly six o'clock in the morning. Alethia had barely slept at all. She hurriedly grabbed her suitcase and headed down the stairs of the apartment complex. It was a muggy sixty degrees outside with the clouds overhead suggesting it might rain.

Odeza got out of the sleek, expensive-looking black car to open the trunk for her and lift her suitcase in.

"Good morning," he said to her.

"Good morning," she replied.

They stood in awkward silence for a few seconds before Odeza walked around and opened the passenger door for Alethia.

Inside the car, Odeza slid his unlocked cellphone into her hands as he turned on the Bluetooth radio.

"You can go through my music. See if you deem anything acceptable to listen to," he offered.

Alethia easily found the music app on his phone. It felt like an impropriety to have Odeza's unlocked phone in her hands. Odeza smoothly pulled away from the curb, and they drove in silence as Alethia scrolled through his music.

"That bad, huh?" Odeza smirked after a few minutes had gone by.

"I don't know any of these songs," Alethia admitted as she continued to scroll.

"Here," Odeza said as he gently took the phone out of her hand. He easily navigated the device as he monitored the street with one hand on the wheel, glancing down every few seconds until he found what he was looking for. He slid his phone into the cupholder as a song began playing. It was a jazzy tune with lo-fi beats, the high quality of speakers in the sedan doing it justice.

"As I'm sure you read in my email by now, we'll be going to three different districts. The first will be District 17. The flight's about five hours. Have you been to SeaPoint Bay?"

Alethia turned to Odeza as she replied, "Is that a real question?" *Had she been to SeaPoint Bay.* He might as well have asked her if she had met the Chief Commander of the United Districts of the New World.

SeaPoint Bay was one of the most coveted travel destinations and had been since long before the reorganization of the new world in the 2050s. District 17 was a very popular place for tourists. Alethia, in fact, had *not* ever been there, but she of course knew of its powder-white sandy coastline backed by rugged, steep mountains, the cities and towns built into the mountains, and the charming cobblestone streets. It was said to be a paradise.

Since Odeza hadn't indulged her sarcastic snark, Alethia asked another, more sincere question. "Why have *I* been asked to tour Ascensio's other facilities?"

"I told you," Odeza replied simply, shrugging. "One of the new quality control measures Ascensio has come up with is to have a handful of different employees at different times survey the sites to provide feedback. We're always striving for improvement. We want new, fresh eyes to give an unbiased perspective. Seeing as you're new, you're the lucky contender."

"But what is it exactly that I'm supposed to give feedback on? Paint color? Cafeteria food quality? Patient care?"

"You may make comments on any of the above," Odeza said and glanced over at her. "This isn't some kind of test, if that's what you're wondering. It's a perk of working for one of the world's most cutting-edge companies. You're allowed to enjoy it."

Alethia settled back into her seat, pondering what he had said.

"We'll see about that," she muttered.

14. ODEZA
JANUARY 2073

Their flight landed at SeaPoint Regional Airport at 6:00 PM local time. With Ascensio's flier benefits, they were in and out of the airport in a breeze. This was Odeza's third time visiting SeaPoint Bay, but he did not believe he'd ever get used to it. It truly was heaven on earth.

As they stepped outside, a salty breeze laced with the aroma of lemons and sweet pea washed over them. The sun would be setting in an hour or so, but it was still warm out. The airport gave only a hint of the view of the ocean that they would see in full splendor at their lodging.

Odeza peaked over at Alethia. Her golden-brown eyes were wide, glistening as she took in their surroundings. She caught him looking at her and beamed.

"It's beautiful here," she said.

Odeza returned her smile. "Hungry?" he asked.

"Starving," she replied.

Odeza chuckled, "Let's go check in, and then we'll get dinner."

Alethia motioned for him to lead the way.

Ascensio had a longstanding private reservation in SeaPoint Bay at the Blanca Villas and Resort. It was a fifteen-minute cab ride from the airport up the skinny and winding coastal road dotted with homes, timeshares, and resorts.

Odeza guided Alethia through the bungalow's open-air lobby, with its white stone walls, rustic stone floor, plush sofas, and abundant green plants.

"Good evening," he greeted the receptionist at the check-in desk.

The receptionist, whose name tag read *Donna*, obviously recognized Odeza. As soon as she saw him, she immediately straightened her posture and offered him a wide-eyed smile. "Good evening Mr. Speer. And Ms. . . . ?"

"Burkshire," Alethia confirmed before Odeza could make the introduction.

"We have a reservation for the Primrose Suite," Odeza said as he passed her the black company credit card with Ascensio's signa of silver ascending spiral stairs.

"Excellent. It's a pleasure to meet you," Donna said to Alethia and looked back to Odeza before adding quietly with a knowing look, "Would you like roses and champagne sent to the master suite, sir?"

Odeza watched as Alethia's eyes nearly popped out. Her cheeks turned rose-colored as she abruptly looked away. This was not the first time he had brought a woman to the Primrose Suite.

Odeza cleared his throat. "This is my colleague. There will be no need."

Now it was Donna's turn to blush. "Apologies, sir and madam." She handed them each a key card. "Let me know if there is anything at all you need during your stay."

As they walked along the stone path through the center courtyard full of exotic and aromatic plants, Alethia didn't so much as look at Odeza.

He stopped just outside of the entry to their private villa. "You know, I should have asked you first," he baited.

"Asked me what?" Alethia replied, looking at him warily.

"Did you want the roses and champagne?" He smirked at her.

She gave him an exasperated look and threw up her hands before crossing them tightly over her chest and glaring at him.

Odeza only smirked again before opening the door for her.

15. ALETHIA
JANUARY 2073

Alethia marched passed Odeza, muttering to herself, *One week. One week with this insufferable man.* She got about three feet before she froze.

She found herself in what could have been a mansion. The front room was a sprawling lounge. There were sofas of deep red and gold stacked with fat pillows. The stone floor stretched to the far side of the room where a wall of glass doors opened into a private courtyard full of lush foliage. A granite bar with cushioned stools was tucked into the corner of the room to her right. The room was full of artwork depicting the beautiful landscape that surrounded them.

"Allow me to show you to your room," Odeza said.

At a loss for words, Alethia merely nodded and followed.

He led her down a broad hallway to the right until they reached the double doors at the very end.

"Seeing as it's your first time in SeaPoint, I thought it only appropriate for you to stay in the master," Odeza said to her as he opened the double doors.

The master bedroom was bigger than Alethia's entire flat back at home. At the center of the room stood a king-size bed with a cherry wood bedframe adorned with intricate carvings along the head and footboard. The bedspread was embroidered with gold thread, as were the multitude of pillows atop it.

To the right of the bed was a private bathing room with a marble tub that would likely fit at least three people. Atop a polished white marble countertop sat a tray with crystal bottles of perfume, lotion, and soap.

Alethia walked back out to the bedroom. On the left side of the room was a sitting room with couches and a fireplace. Odeza stood by a wall of closed curtains, waiting for her. She walked over, and he gazed down at her as he pulled the rope to open the curtains.

Alethia felt her jaw drop. The view outside her window displayed sprawling cliffs along the coastline and the sea beyond. Little stone buildings of every color dotted the cliffside. She could see the sandy white beach far below and the crashing waves bringing in the tide. The sun was just beginning to set over the horizon, leaving the whole scene ablaze in pink and gold.

Alethia gazed out at the scene for some time before turning back. She found Odeza still watching her and felt her cheeks warm.

She looked up into his steel eyes. The soft expression on his face was new to her. He held her gaze for only a moment before snapping back to his usual cadence.

"I'll leave you to get settled," Odeza declared as he made for the doorway. He paused with his hand on the doorknob. "Oh, and Alethia?"

"Yes?" she replied, her voice nearly a whisper.

"You'll want to find a dress to wear for dinner." He eyed her up and down with that stupid smirk he always wore. "It's a *formal* restaurant we'll be eating at."

"I didn't pack *cocktail dresses*, Odeza. I thought this was a *business* trip," she fired back, crossing her arms.

"I figured as much," he said. "You should find what you need in the wardrobe." With that, he shut the door behind him.

Alethia huffed out a breath. She went to the wardrobe and opened the doors. Sure enough, there were dresses hanging in it.

16. ODEZA
JANUARY 2073

Odeza grabbed his luggage from the front room and made his way to the bedroom he would be staying in. He changed into a tux for dinner. His phone rang just as he was adjusting his black tie. He glanced over and sighed—it was Elizabeth.

"Hi Liz," Odeza said, leaning against the doorframe that led to his private bathroom.

"So, have you made it to The Blanca? You're supposed to be checking in with me you, know."

"Yes, we've just now made it," he replied, rolling his eyes. His phone had a tracker on it, so he knew full well that she already knew where they were.

"How was the flight?"

"Long, fine. Nothing out of the ordinary." Odeza examined his fingernails.

"Hmm. How are the rooms? Impeccable I presume?"

"Fantastic, as always, doll," he replied dryly.

"Good." He could hear the jealousy in her voice. "Well, you know what to do, schmooze her until she feels indebted to us." She let out a cackle. "But stay focused and remember why you're *really* on this little *business trip*, mmkay?"

"I know, Liz. I'll check in in the morning, okay?"

"Okay. Bye, darling."

He sighed and rolled out his shoulders. These women were going to be the end of him.

Odeza heard the door to Alethia's room open and close. Her timid footsteps grew closer down the hallway. She passed his room and went out into the front room.

"Odeza?" she called.

He ran his fingers through his hair and straightened his tie before casually walking out to meet her. She was headed for the courtyard. He leaned against the doorway to the hall and watched her look for him, eyeing her in the dress she had chosen. It was a pink and orange floral dress with cupped, off-the-shoulder sleeves.

It hugged her hips slightly but breezed down her legs. The end hem was angled, beginning just above her right knee and tapering down to her left mid-calf.

Alethia was struggling to open the courtyard door. He heard her swear at it. He laughed. "You have to push in, then turn," he called across the room. Alethia whirled around. Odeza delighted in seeing her cheeks pinken as she became flustered.

"I would have figured it out," she said, smoothing the front of her dress, which wasn't ruffled.

"I don't doubt it," he replied. "Ready?"

Alethia nodded.

* * * *

Odeza took Alethia to a little bistro that overlooked the modest harbor of SeaPoint. Sailboats rocked gently in the evening breeze. The sun was now sinking below the sea's horizon, casting long shadows on the powdery sand and smooth cobblestones. Odeza found himself wishing he were here on different pretenses.

Alethia had been even quieter than usual during the cab ride to the restaurant and was now pointedly examining the menu as if it were a great excuse not to have to speak. Odeza cleared his throat.

"The wine here is exquisite," he said, attempting to break the silence.

Alethia raised an eyebrow at him, "Is it? And are we to indulge on the company's dime? I saw your Ascensio credit card earlier."

Odeza couldn't help letting out a laugh. "Well, you wouldn't expect *me* to pay for your drink at this nice restaurant, would you? That would make this a date."

Alethia's eyes bulged and her mouth fell open, yet she seemed to have no words.

"I'm kidding, of course," Odeza said, chuckling at her reaction.

The waiter came around at that moment, and Odeza ordered a bottle of their finest Riesling with their dinner of lobster and linguine, remembering she had ordered that at the Christmas party.

When the waiter brought out the bottle and poured them each a glass, Odeza watched as she took her first sip. Though he knew she tried, she couldn't hide the satisfaction on her face.

"Well?" he asked.

"It's very good," she said with a soft smile and set her glass down. "So. What's the plan for tomorrow?"

"You just don't care for surprises, do you?"

"I like to know what to expect," she countered.

"What's the fun in that?" He took a slow sip of wine and watched her over the rim of his glass. She was becoming annoyed again, and he was enjoying it.

She sighed and looked warily at him. "You really aren't going to tell me?"

"Fine," he drawled, dramatically rolling his eyes. "We will be touring the Ascensio facility here at SeaPoint in the morning. After that, we'll have a little time to be tourists before we catch our next flight."

"Where will we be going next?"

"It's my turn to ask a question," Odeza said, swirling his wine.

Alethia raised her eyebrows.

"Where are you from?" he asked.

"I'm from Desert View. I've lived there all my life, except for the years I was in college." Alethia gazed down at the table as if recalling that time of her life.

"And where did you go to college?"

"I'm sure you already know that," she replied, narrowing her eyes. "I know you've seen my resume. You were on the hiring committee. Or was my application so forgettable?"

Odeza couldn't tell if she was offended or if she was teasing him. She wasn't supposed to make him squirm—that was the game *he* was playing. He had, in fact, seen her resume, and he truly did not remember.

"I see a lot of applications," he finally responded.

"Hmm," was all she said, pressing her lips together.

"So, you aren't going to tell me?" Odeza pressed.

"Now look who's got all the questions. It's my turn to ask one. Where are *you* from?"

"Ah . . . " Odeza leaned back in his chair, sizing her up. "I am from Northern Dearsfield. It's in District 5."

"So, you didn't grow up in the desert? What brought you out there?"

"I came out to work at Ascensio headquarters in my early twenties." That was a time in Odeza's life he'd be happy to forget.

"What's it like where you're from?" Alethia placed a fist under her chin and leaned forward, genuinely interested.

The scene of his childhood home flashed before Odeza's eyes. Scratched, old hardwood floors. Red flannel curtains. His mom always kept the kitchen clean. She'd had to sweep daily because of the broken glass bottles ...

"It's, um, it's cold there." Odeza blinked away the memory. "But enough about me. Back to your college days. Any *crazy* stories?" He refilled both of their glasses.

Alethia watched him, huffing out a laugh at his question. "I think we both know the answer to that."

"What is *that* supposed to mean?" Odeza raised one eyebrow.

"Oh, come *on*," Alethia replied. "I can tell what you believe to be true about me. That I'm boring. Cautious. Type *A*."

"Well, *are* you?"

There was a momentary pause before they both laughed. The wine was doing its work. He could tell she was loosening up, but he was too. Odeza became aware that he was almost ... enjoying himself. He looked back to Alethia and found her looking at him. Their eyes locked briefly before she looked away.

"We should probably get back," Alethia said. "Early start and all."

"Ah," Odeza said, as if solving a puzzle.

"What?"

"You *are* boring," he said, and winked at her as he gathered the check to pay.

17. ALETHIA
JANUARY 2073

Ascensio, Inc.'s headquarters at SeaPoint Bay was vastly different from its headquarters back home. Alethia stepped out of the cab and onto the cobblestone path that led to the property. There were large willow trees along a tall, ornate wrought iron gate that blocked the view of the building. Odeza had explained that this facility was a gated community to provide optimal security for the patients. When Alethia inquired what scary things could possibly pose a threat to the residents of SeaPoint Bay, of all places, he dryly replied that tourists can get very wild here.

While Alethia found Odeza's response to be a quip remark, she quickly dropped it as they walked past the gates and the willows. The grounds of the property floored her. She thought to herself that she'd be absolutely okay with living in a gated community this beautiful.

The long and winding cobblestone path stretched up to the grand building that resembled a castle from hundreds of years ago. There were arched windows, stained glass, and a tall bell tower. The immaculate grassy lawn was covered in clusters of shrubs, wildflowers, and trees. A koi pond was nestled in one of the groves and a large stone fountain was trickling up ahead. And the *smell* . . . Alethia closed her eyes and deeply inhaled the scent of roses, gardenias, freshly mowed grass, and morning dew. If heaven was a place on earth, Alethia believed she might be glimpsing it.

"Enjoying yourself?" Odeza asked her.

Alethia looked up at his smug face. "Well, I *was*," she replied, doing her best to convey her distaste for him.

"By all means, don't let me intrude on your gawking."

"I was not *gawking*!"

"You were gawking."

"Whatever."

They were approaching the entrance of the facility, and Alethia spied an older woman in tan slacks and a pink floral blouse coming out to greet them. Her curly grey hair was in a loose bun and there was a pleasant smile on her tan face.

"Welcome," she said as Alethia and Odeza made their way up the sprawling stone steps. Alethia noted her accent reflected the dialect of the locals. "Mr. Speer, always a pleasure. And you must be Ms. Burkshire. I've heard so much about you."

Alethia was taken aback by her last statement. What exactly had this woman across the districts heard about her? When they reached the top of the steps, Alethia shook the woman's hand and gave her best attempt at a confident smile.

"I'm Dr. Leone."

"It's a pleasure to meet you," Alethia replied. "It's very beautiful here," she added.

"I'm so glad you think so. Hopefully you will feel the same about the interior of our facility. Are you ready for your tour?"

"Absolutely," Alethia said, smiling at the woman.

"Have *fun*," Odeza drawled, flicking his eyebrows up and down at Alethia.

"You're not coming with us?" Alethia blurted. She immediately regretted opening her mouth.

"Miss me, will you?" Odeza chirped. "Don't worry, she won't keep you away from me for *too* long."

Alethia was appalled at his manner of speaking, especially in front of a complete stranger who was also a work associate. She looked to Dr. Leone for her reaction, but the woman just smiled at her in a knowing way. Alethia felt herself blushing in embarrassment.

"This way, dear." Dr Leone gestured toward the front doors, saving Alethia from another moment of the awkward exchange.

They stepped into a grand entrance where the ceiling soared high above them. Staying true to the historical building, Alethia felt like she was stepping back in time. The facility obviously had updated electricity, yet there were preserved sconces on the walls. Paintings of the countryside, secured in heavy-looking ornate frames, adorned the lobby walls. Deep red sofas and wooden end tables were off to the side. Alethia could see a more modern-looking check-in area ahead, and two large stone archways on either side of the room with corridors going who-knew where.

Dr. Leone nodded to the receptionists at the check-in desk as she led Alethia down the corridor to the left. The long stone hallway, decorated with more sconces and paintings, stretched ahead with wooden doors to their right and windows spaced out to their left, overlooking the beautiful grounds.

Absorbed in her surroundings, Alethia hadn't registered how quiet it had been since their entrance. But she suddenly realized that Dr. Leone, as pleasant as she seemed, wasn't saying anything. Alethia suddenly felt compelled to fill the silence.

"So, um, have you worked for Ascensio for a while?" she asked.

"Oh, yes," Dr. Leone murmured with a small smile. "I was among the first, back when Ascensio was just beginning. We've come a long way since then."

"I can imagine," Alethia offered.

"These doors ahead will lead us into our residents' common room."

Residents. Not patients. Alethia took note of this.

Despite the old age of the facility building, signs of modern upgrades were becoming more evident. Dr. Leone pulled the key card attached to a retractable badge holder at her waste and scanned it on the reader to the right of the door. There was a click as she pushed open the heavy oak door.

Inside the common room, there was a glossy wooden floor with large decorative area rugs placed underneath brown leather sofas and matching chairs. Lush green plants hung from the ceiling and sat in painted terracotta planters all around the room. There were residents playing board games with each other, reading, socializing, and some watching TV. They all looked ... happy. Content. Normal ... "normal" as in not sick, Alethia surmised.

These "residents" looked vastly different from the "patients" at headquarters. None of them seemed to pay any mind to Alethia as they walked through the room. French double doors stood open on the south wall, letting in the fresh air. Alethia spied more residents outside on a terrace, each positioned before a canvas and easel, as an instructor led them through a painting lesson.

Alethia smiled. It warmed her heart to see these people, who undoubtedly suffered from dark internal struggles, thriving in such a beautiful environment. All too often, she saw people suffering, in desperate need of relief from their circumstances or mental state. She was eager to uncover the secret to SeaPoint's remarkably effective approach to treatment.

"This is . . . incredible," Alethia said, turning to Dr. Leone.

The doctor smiled. "I'm glad you think so."

"I would love to talk more . . . perhaps in private," Alethia said quietly, not wanting the residents to overhear her talking about them. "I've never seen such successful results."

"Of course, all in good time," she promised with a wink.

As the tour continued, Alethia was led through the resident living quarters, the dining area, and a few of the therapy rooms. Each room was just as beautiful as the last, with fine artwork, cozy furniture, open windows letting in the warm breeze, and more thriving residents.

Throughout their tour, Dr. Leone told Alethia about the array of cutting-edge therapies available to the residents. They were encouraged to engage in art, play or listen to music, undergo talk therapy with seasoned psychiatrists, and partake in various other activities designed to make the residents feel good about themselves and their skills.

"But the most effective treatment of all, by far," Dr. Leone said as she was walking Alethia back to the front lobby to end their tour, "is the revolutionary medicine that has taken Ascensio's scientists decades to fine-tune. We have created not just a *treatment* for mental illness, but a cure."

Alethia was dumbfounded by this information. "I'm confused . . . I am just hearing about this. Why has there been no information about this at our other headquarters?"

"SeaPoint is the first facility to put the new medication to use. Now, I don't want you to worry; they are not blind test subjects in an experiment," Dr. Leone chuckled. "Every patient who has taken the serum has consented and knows that it is a new treatment that we are monitoring."

Alethia's brow furrowed. She still felt like this was a secret that had been kept from her. She wondered how it could even be possible to create a *cure* for mental suffering.

Alethia became aware that Dr. Leone was watching her and that she had yet to respond. She carefully molded her face to mimicked amazement and proclaimed, "That's unbelievable."

18. ODEZA
JANUARY 2073

After her tour, Odeza took Alethia into town. They strolled along cobblestone streets lined with colorful shops selling candies, flowers, and a menagerie of other tourist trinkets. The sun was warm on their backs. He observed Alethia as she walked beside him, trying not to stare at how the sunlight seemed to turn her hair golden as it shimmered in the light.

She hadn't said much since he returned to the facility to collect her. The entire time they had been walking, he could have sworn that her brow had been furrowed and her mind was somewhere else.

"Penny for your thoughts?" he asked.

She slowly looked at him as if she'd forgotten he was there. "I've been trying to figure out whether I've been given *information* today—or let in on a *secret*."

"Sorry?" Odeza asked, puzzled.

"Considering your rank is much higher than mine, I don't doubt you're already aware that they have some kind of alleged *cure* for mental illnesses in there?"

"Ah. That." Odeza put his hands in his pockets and looked up at the sky for a moment, then back at her accusatory gaze. "It's not a secret. And, as you put it, it's an *alleged* cure. It seems revolutionary, absolutely, but it does need to be tested."

"On our patients."

"On very willing ones."

"But why am I just now hearing about this?"

"Listen, Alethia," Odeza began softly, mindful of their public location. "Ascensio is on the brink of something very big. This could change . . . everything about the wellbeing of humanity. It's not a secret per say . . . but we regard trust and loyalty very highly. We can't just throw this information out on a new employee's first day of training. We have to make sure they're in this for the long hall, and that such information will be kept—"

"—a secret?" Alethia interjected.

"*Sensitive.* Until more published studies are available," he corrected.

Alethia looked forward. He could tell from her face that she was digesting the information.

"You seem upset," Odeza commented.

"No, I'm not *upset*. I'm just ... I don't know what I am. Still just processing how such a thing could be possible. I mean, have there been any negative effects? How long has the testing been going on for? And is this the only facility testing the drug?"

Odeza hadn't realized Alethia would have so many questions. Concern was growing in his gut at her reaction. The point of this trip was *not* to return home with her questioning Ascensio's ethics.

"Look." Odeza stopped, placing his hands on Alethia's shoulders, and turning her gently so she would look at him. Her deep brown eyes had flecks of green and gold in them as her face turned up to meet his and the sun beat down on it. "I promise you this is something good. Tell me you saw even a single person in that facility that looked miserable or was suffering, and we'll go back there right now and break the doors down."

Alethia blinked and looked at him as if for the first time. He could see in her eyes that she was startled by the lack of sarcasm in his voice that he usually hid behind. For the first time, he had abandoned the banter and teasing that was so amusing to him when he was around her. He recognized that, right now, she needed to see him as someone other than a cad. And, as he looked at her, Odeza found himself wondering which of the two personas was more of a charade.

"Everyone I saw looked . . . happy," Alethia conceded. She pursed her lips to the side in contemplation and broke their intense eye contact. "I can see your point that it would be sensitive information for the time being," she continued, saying the words as though she were tasting them for truth. "I think it's phenomenal, if it *does* truly end up working," she finished her thought with certainty, looking back up at him.

Odeza recognized, in that moment, how much Alethia cared for people. It had always been obvious that she cared, but he hadn't realized how *deeply*.

He cleared his throat and resumed walking.

"I agree," he said.

19. ALETHIA
JANUARY 2073

Their next flight touched down at 1:30 PM in District 11. It was actually a proper *winter* there. A fresh blanket of snow covered the peaks and valleys of the rugged land. Alethia gazed out the window of their rented SUV as Odeza drove them up a precarious road with towering pines on either side.

Alethia had found, for the second time, that she had not packed efficiently for this trip. She had known they would be visiting Allsbrook Village in the mountain district, but she had never lived outside of the desert, so she hadn't had a clue that a sweater and leggings wouldn't cut it in the winter there. Odeza had immediately taken her to one of the shopping outlets near the airport and bought her a puffy, faux fur-lined coat and snow boots.

"Are we ... staying somewhere all the way up here?" Alethia asked. It seemed like they were getting closer and closer to the very top of one of the towering mountains. Every turn on the winding road made Alethia's stomach clench as she tried not to think about what would happen if their tires slid.

"Not exactly," Odeza smirked.

"Excuse me?" Alethia raised an eyebrow at him. "Then where *exactly* are we going?"

"We're going snowboarding. Or skiing, if you prefer."

"*What?* Odeza, I've never been skiing or snowboarding in my entire life. I've never left the desert, remember?" Panic rose in Alethia's chest. Her eyes burned holes into the side of Odeza's annoyingly handsome face as he just continued to smugly look ahead.

"I figured as much." He shrugged and stole a glance her way before locking his eyes back on the slippery terrain. "But I have."

"Oh great, I'm very happy for you. I guess I'm supposed to just watch you from the car?" Alethia scoffed.

"Well, you certainly could, but that sounds *very* boring," Odeza replied. The small coy smile still danced on his lips.

Alethia crossed her arms and continued to glare at him.

"What? I thought you might enjoy a lesson," he said in a daring tone.

Alethia flopped back into her seat and huffed a sigh. Rubbing her temples, she muttered, "This is the weirdest business trip I've ever heard of."

Odeza laughed and turned into a small muddy, snow-covered parking lot with cars parked haphazardly due to the lack of any kind of pre-designated parking space. Alethia tried to keep her pulse from hammering. Fear crawled up from her gut into her throat. She didn't like heights. She didn't like trying something new with someone she didn't know very well. She didn't want to do this.

"Odeza, I don't have any of the gear required—"

"Would you relax?" he chided, shifting the car into park. "We can rent everything you need here at the slope."

Alethia swallowed hard. Odeza looked over at her, but she refrained from meeting his eyes.

"Come on, give it a try—just one try—and if you hate it, we can leave," he said more gently, seemingly realizing the extent of her discomfort. As if to ease the building tension in the car, he teased, "You're not afraid of falling in front of me, are you?"

Yes, she absolutely was.

"Of course not!" she shot back.

He raised his eyebrows and tilted his head.

"What's the point of this, though? Why do we need to do this?" she demanded, heat rising to her face. She felt embarrassed to be scared of something in front of him.

"The point is to have fun," he replied simply.

The idea of looking weak in front of Odeza Speer was intolerable to Alethia. She would rather suck it up and pretend she could handle it than hear an ounce of pity in his voice.

"Fine, let's go," She said firmly and opened her car door.

* * * *

They quickly rented gear, both opting for snowboards, and bought half-day tickets. Odeza informed

Alethia that, this late in the day, they only had a few hours left to be on the mountain. Alethia was perfectly okay with that.

The ski lift bench swayed as it moseyed its way higher and higher along the path to where they would dismount. Alethia held on to the bar in front of her as tightly as she could with the annoyingly thick gloves Odeza had made her wear. While it made it a challenge to grasp anything, she had to admit they were warm.

Getting on the lift was awkward with one booted foot strapped into the snowboard and the other free so she could shuffle herself around. She had felt like an idiot and had fallen over twice during the awkward shuffle before they'd even been scooped up by the lift. Alethia could see the top nearing and suddenly realized she had absolutely no idea how to get off this thing.

She swung her helmeted head toward Odeza, who looked as relaxed as could be on a swaying bench thirty feet in the air. Sensing her concern as the lift crept closer to where they would dismount, Odeza explained,

"We're going to lift this bar up soon, and you're going to want to scoot forward in the chair. Put your free foot on the board." He demonstrated, turning his board to point in front of him. "And when I say so, push yourself off the bench and try to straighten yourself as you slide forward." Odeza's voice was calm and reassuring. It was all Alethia could do to nod and concentrate on the instructions he had given her.

They were maybe twenty feet from the top. Odeza lifted the safety bar. They both scooted forward and turned, pointing their boards, as they approached the top.

"*Now*, push off," Odeza instructed.

Alethia pushed off from the lift and felt her board make contact with the ground. She wobblily slid forward a few feet and flung her arms out in a feeble attempt to steady herself before falling flat on her ass.

Odeza was there in an instant to help her up. She expected him to make fun of her fall, but instead he said, "You okay? That was good for your first attempt."

"Yeah, I'm fine," she replied. *First attempt*. So, she'd have to do that again? She cringed.

They scooted themselves away from the dismounting area to properly strap into the snowboards. Odeza explained to her that the front of her board was her toe edge, and the back was her heel edge, accurately

DISSIPATION

reflecting where her feet were strapped. He modeled the maneuvers to her as he explained. He told her how to control her speed and stop herself by using her edges to dig into the snow, that the idea is to snake your way down the mountain by alternating edges.

"Ready to give it a try?" Odeza asked.

No, she thought.

"Okay," she agreed, and then frowned. "How am I supposed to get up?" Her backside was on the ground with her knees bent and her board out in front of her.

Odeza chuckled.

"*Do not* laugh at me." Alethia glared up at him through her goggles.

"I wouldn't dare," Odeza said, biting his smile back.

He modeled for her how she could either rock herself forward and push up to stand, or flip onto her knees and push herself up that way. Trying to flip herself over with a five-foot board stuck to her feet sounded like an embarrassment she didn't want to add to today's list. She attempted to rock herself forward and stand. Had Odeza not been right there to steady her, she probably would have fallen on her face.

Odeza firmly held her arms with ease. His toned build was like a solid rock in front of her. Since she was further up on the incline, she was closer to his eye level than she was used to. She looked through the orange tinted goggles he wore and into his bright grey eyes framed by black lashes.

She had been so in her head worrying about, well, *everything* that had to do with learning how to snowboard, she hadn't realized that Odeza had been . . . actually very nice to her, oddly. He'd been patient instead of mocking. Gentle instead of arrogant. It was almost like he was trying extra hard to be on his best behavior so she wouldn't have a completely awful first experience. As if he actually *cared* about teaching her and showing her a good time. The combination of his hold on her arms and the close proximity of him made her stomach flutter for an entirely different reason than the daunting slope before them.

Throughout the afternoon, Alethia found herself loosening up. She estimated that she fell probably at least a hundred times and could feel the soreness creeping over her whole body, but she actually felt really good. There were a few moments of sliding smoothly onto her edges without falling that pumped her with the high of gaining a difficult new skill. She felt accomplished, even though she was far from Odeza's mastery.

She watched him glide and turn with ease. Despite the obvious speed he was capable of, he always waited for her and offered her encouragement.

They were almost down from their last run of the day when unexpected confidence surged in Alethia. She guided the tip of her board towards the incline and slowly eased into it. Suddenly, she was flying faster than she had yet to go.

Oh shit, she thought, falling into a panic as her speed kept increasing. She instinctively tried to lean back, forgetting everything she'd been taught today—and went down. Hard. She felt her body being yanked by her board twisting her as she toppled over herself twice before finally sliding to a stop flat on her back. *Ouch.*

"Alethia!" Odeza shouted.

He had been behind her because of her request to watch her for errors before she stupidly decided to go full ham down the mountain. She could hear him racing down to her on his board. Snow flew as he sliced into a stop and dropped to his knees before her.

"Are you okay?" he breathed. The tone of his voice dripped in terror. His eyes darted across her body, checking for any obvious injuries.

"I'm . . . " she started as his eyes snapped to hers intensely, " . . . an idiot."

Alethia watched Odeza's shoulders fall in relief as his mouth dropped open. She began giggling. Perhaps it was the adrenaline from thinking she was going to die a few moments ago, or perhaps it was the shock on Odeza's normally schooled features, but Alethia couldn't help but laugh.

"I think we need to have you checked for a concussion," Odeza said, with concern growing on his face. "Can you get up on your own?"

"I don't know," Alethia got out in between bouts of her untimely laughing fit.

Odeza shook his head and huffed a laugh of his own before he said, "Okay, let's get you up."

20. ALETHIA
JANUARY 2073

The cold winter sun was starting its early decent behind the mountains as they made their way back down the winding, icy road. Snow crunched under the tires. Golden beams of light peaked through the pine trees and made the snow sparkle. The air at this altitude was crisp and thin and fresh. Alethia sighed, trying to capture all the beauty the mountain had to offer, knowing she'd soon be leaving.

Alethia and Odeza hadn't spoken much since leaving the ski slope, but it didn't feel awkward for a change. It had been a long day, and they were both tired. Alethia found herself, once again, without any idea where they were staying and what the plan would be for tomorrow, but she was too exhausted to make a fuss about it.

The ride to their lodging was much shorter than Alethia anticipated. They had not driven all the way back down to town as she had expected. Instead, Odeza had turned off on another winding road along the mountain. They were now pulling into the driveway of a very fancy, very expensive-looking house nestled on the cliff edge among the trees. She would have called it a cabin because of the gigantic, polished logs it appeared to be built out of, but the grandeur of the home contradicted the notion of what Alethia pictured a log cabin to be.

"Um. Whose house is this?" Alethia blurted.

"Ours, for the night," Odeza retorted as he put the car in park and unbuckled his seatbelt.

Alethia rolled her eyes. *Of course* he would not just give her a straight answer. She unbuckled her seatbelt and opened the passenger door. Odeza was already there, offering her a hand to step down from the SUV. She raised her eyebrows at his chivalrous gesture.

"Trust me, you're going to want a hand," he explained with a smirk.

Huffing, Alethia took his hand and stepped down from the vehicle. Fiery pain shot down the hamstring and ankle of her right foot as it connected with the driveway. She gasped, her leg nearly giving out. Odeza quickly caught her, placing his free arm underneath her left armpit. They were now in a semi-embrace, and the smell of Odeza's cologne caressed her senses. He smelled of teakwood and spice. His arm was warm and solid where it connected with her. Their eyes met for a brief moment before she pulled herself to her feet and stepped away.

"Thanks," she murmured.

Odeza ran his fingers through his hair and cleared his throat. "Told you so."

He grabbed their bags from the car, and they walked up the cleared stone pathway. Alethia wondered if they were alone, considering *someone* would've had to shovel the snow. Odeza set the bags down and punched in a code for the door. It unlocked with a click, and he opened it, gesturing for her to enter.

Alethia surmised that the normalcy she kept expecting of this so-called business trip would never show itself. This was more of a vacation than anything, she thought as she walked into the large front room.

A grand stone fireplace climbed all the way up to the vaulted ceiling. Gleaming wooden beams framed the interior. A black leather sofa sat in front of the fireplace, which was somehow already lit, with matching leather recliners on either side. A heavy wooden coffee table and matching end tables completed the set. A gigantic bear rug sat underneath, and white, fuzzy blankets were casually draped over the sofa. Iron figures of bears and moose adorned the mantle with pinecones interspersed. The wall parallel to the entrance was primarily made of glass windows stretching all the way to the pitched ceiling. Alethia's eyes grew wide as she walked closer to the view.

There was a sprawling wooden deck with a sunken hot tub and polished pine lounge chairs facing the adjacent mountain peaks and pine trees dusted with vibrant white snow. There were no other houses visible, just rugged, unadulterated wilderness.

She was stunned. She didn't know what to think or do, so she just stood there, staring at the final sparkles on the snow as the sun descended behind the peaks. She jumped as Odeza closed the front door. It was *so* quiet here.

"Do you want to pick your room, or should I drop your bags in the closest one?" He asked her.

What was she doing letting him carry her bags? She was perfectly capable. She walked over to him with her best attempt at masking her screaming muscles.

"Sorry—I can take them—" she started.

He didn't hand the bags over, just tossed his head to the side and gave her a look that said, "*Really?*"

She crossed her arms and returned a look that said, "*Yes, really.*"

He narrowed his eyes and said nothing as he simply just walked right past her.

He was so *annoying*.

"I said I could carry them," she insisted uselessly to his back as she followed.

He plopped her luggage on a huge bed with a sturdy pine frame that matched the aesthetic of the furniture in the front room. The bedroom was cozy and grand, like the rest of the house. *Wait*, she thought, remembering she'd never gotten an answer before, *whose house is this?* She repeated her question aloud to Odeza.

"This house," he said, turning around to face her, "belongs to Ascensio. It's used all the time by employees traveling to the Allsbrook site for business. Sometimes it's even used as a reward benefit for employees to vacation at. And to answer the next question that *I'm sure* you have, knowing how observant you are, there's no one else here, currently. We have a cleaning and maintenance crew outsourced to maintain the lot while it's not in use. They even stock the fridge and bar. Speaking of, I'm sure you're starving after our . . . eventful afternoon," he said, eyeing her sagging posture.

She was indeed starving.

"I could eat," she shrugged.

After raiding some snacks from the pantry, they settled on a frozen lasagna they had found in the freezer for dinner. Odeza had said he was a lousy cook, and she admitted the same. Odeza set the oven to preheat.

"I may not be able to cook worth a damn, but I can make a drink," he offered.

"Sure," Alethia obliged. "Surprise me." The two not-quite-strangers, not-quite-friends had all evening to be alone together in this massive house. Might as well take the edge off, she figured.

She watched him go to the bar on the other side of the kitchen. She sat on one of the bar stools and scooted up to the granite kitchen island. The sizable kitchen was just around the corner from the entrance, and she had a full view of the fireplace and the windows looking out to the deck.

It was pitch black out there now with no city lights to illuminate the night. Small solar lights lit the deck just enough for one to see where they were walking, but beyond that it was a dark void. It gave Alethia the eerie feeling she was being watched by a bear or a wolf or whatever else lived in the forest around the home.

Odeza returned with two short glasses containing an amber liquid and garnished with an orange slice.

"Cheers," Odeza said as he handed her the glass and clinked it with his own.

She took a sip. The unmistakable burn of whiskey kissed her throat. The drink was smooth, however, and she took another sip.

"Thanks," she said, offering him a smile.

Odeza nodded and sat beside her.

"I have to say, I'm a little confused . . . well, by all of this," Alethia confided as she gestured around the room.

"It's what we like to call a kitchen," Odeza quipped.

"Are you always a smartass?" Alethia threw back at him, narrowing her eyes.

Odeza tapped his chin. "Come to think of it, yes," he said and smiled at her. When she did not smile back, he drawled, "*Care* to elaborate what you mean?"

"I'm talking about this trip, Odeza. It's more of a lavish vacation than anything. I just . . . don't understand why I'm here. I know you said I'm supposed to be getting familiar with the other facilities but what's with all the luxurious lodging and *excursions*?"

Odeza eyed her for a long moment as if deciding whether he was going to answer her. "Given the opportunity to experience the perks of working for this company, most people wouldn't be so unwilling to just enjoy it," he replied carefully.

Alethia frowned, her mouth falling open. "I'm not trying to come off as ungrateful," she faltered.

"I know," Odeza said quietly. "You *are* allowed to enjoy it, though."

"I am," she assured him. "I never thought I would get to see so much of the world, it is an *amazing* opportunity . . . It's just a lot. And there seems to be a lot of play and not a lot of work," she finished.

"Hey, work hard, play hard," Odeza countered. "And *you*," he added, "have been working very hard, from what I hear."

Alethia considered his response. It wasn't exactly an answer.

"It's almost like you don't think you deserve to have a little fun," he remarked, draining the last of his glass.

Did she feel that way? Alethia hadn't considered that. This whole trip, she had been trying to figure out why she of all people deserved to be whisked across the country, fearing some kind of ulterior motive was behind it. Could this really all be a reward? An opportunity few received? Or maybe this was a customary tradition for Ascensio. They obviously had the money to send people about. She realized Odeza was looking at her, waiting for a response.

"Worthiness," she said. "I recall that being the topic of discussion on our first encounter." She said, recalling the awkward interrogation by him during the orientation challenges. She drained her own glass and set it on the counter.

"Ah, our first encounter," Odeza mused. "*That* is a completely different topic of discussion."

Alethia could feel her inhibitions slipping thanks to the alcohol. "Why were you so rude to me that day?" she boldly asked.

Odeza started, obviously taken aback. He looked at her with an unreadable expression before saying in his usual nonchalant tone, "I think I'm going to need another drink for that one."

She slid her glass to him. "As do I."

"You wanna learn how to make it?" he asked. Was he changing the subject? She supposed it would be rude to refuse.

"Sure," she said with feigned enthusiasm. As she got up from the chair, her body reminded her that it was enormously bent out of shape, and she couldn't hide her grimace.

"You seem . . . not okay," Odeza observed.

"I'm fine," Alethia lied.

"Where does it hurt?"

"My legs hurt from the snowboarding practice, but my back got pretty twisted up when I fell. Well, when I fell the *last* time. My neck and shoulders are stiff from some of the other falls," she admitted sheepishly, then immediately felt like she had overshared.

"Right. So, everywhere," Odeza said, offering her an apologetic smile. "I guess I didn't realize how beat up you were getting. You . . . hide your pain well. I wouldn't've had us keep going if I had known—"

"I was enjoying myself," Alethia interrupted. "I had a good time, and honestly, I'm fine." It seemed Alethia was trying to convince Odeza *and* herself of this. She hoped tomorrow wouldn't involve much physical activity.

"Well. Lucky for you, there is a hot tub right out those doors," Odeza reminded her, his tone still sounding apologetic. "*And* the lasagna needs an hour to cook anyways, so now's as good a time as any."

"Alright," Alethia agreed. It did sound heavenly.

* * * *

Alethia found herself *again* lacking the appropriate attire for this non-business business trip. She figured she would have needed dress pants, not a bathing suit. She had little choice of what to wear in the hot tub other than a sports bra and spandex shorts she had packed on the off chance she'd be able to squeeze in a run before their daily obligations. That certainly hadn't happened, and the thought of running now amplified the pain in her legs.

Thankfully, there was a fuzzy robe hanging in the bathroom that she used to cover herself on her way out to the hot tub. It felt uncomfortable to be in this little clothing, let alone how it would have felt to be in a bathing suit around Odeza. It was the sheer agony of her body that made her decide she could live with the discomfort.

Odeza was nowhere in sight as she crossed the living room. Alethia pushed open the door to the deck and was blasted with the freezing night air. She quickly made her way to the steaming hot tub and eased herself in. Odeza had taken off the cover for her and started the jets. She was immediately glad about her decision to get in.

The hot water embraced her and soothed her muscles as she gently flexed them in the water. The pressure of the jets on her lower back and feet made her melt. Alethia looked up at the night sky and let out a contented sigh. The cloud of her breath intermingled with the water's steam, drifting up to those blazing stars.

Alethia heard the door open behind her and she turned to find Odeza, shirtless and in swim trunks, carrying their refilled drinks. She quickly averted her eyes from his bare torso, but one look was enough. Alethia's stomach muscles tightened as she knew that image would remain with her for a long time.

He was sinfully attractive. Always covered in suit and tie, she had no idea he was so fit. He wasn't ripped like a bodybuilder, but he was all lean muscle under velvet-soft skin. Alethia had to force her mind to shut down the urge to see what that skin felt like. To feel his muscles flex under her fingertips.

"I couldn't leave you all by your lonesome out here," he said stepping into the hot tub. "You know, there are bears in these woods."

Great, yes, she thought, *think about bears. Think about a bear chasing you through the woods. Not about Odeza's arms sweeping you up and rescuing you from the bear and—shit.*

Alethia took her glass from him, avoiding eye contact. "Have you ever seen one? A bear, I mean. Have you ever seen a bear?" Her words tumbled clumsily out of her mouth.

"Of course," he replied. She continued *not* looking at him, but she could hear him draping his long arms on the edge of the tub. He had sat a respectable distance away, but she was so, *so* aware of his nearness. He continued, "I used to go hunting a lot with my dad, back before—well, when I was young."

Something about the way his tone had shifted made Alethia wonder if there was a lot more to that story. She knew so little about this man's life.

"Did you hunt bears?" she asked, completely ignorant about anything related to hunting.

He chuckled. "No, we hunted for elk mostly. The occasional deer."

"Hmm," she mused. "I never would have pinned you as a hunter."

"Why is that?"

"Well, you're a suit and tie guy in my mind. That's all I've known you to be in the short time we've been acquainted. Well, that and a snowboarder apparently," she added, finally looking at him. That was a mistake.

The darkness of the night made Odeza's pupils dilate, causing him to somehow look more innocent, gentler. The dim glow of the lights in the hot tub reflected in them as his gray irises shone the deepest shade of grey. His posture was relaxed. He tilted his head to the side in curiosity at her comment. Alethia realized they were both intently examining the other's face and she broke her stare.

"I'm sure there are many things about me that don't present on the surface," Odeza finally replied. Alethia immediately wondered if she had offended him. She took a long drink from her glass.

"Well, maybe you could tell me a few of them," she suggested, stealing another glance.

Who was this pensive and demure Odeza? And why did she feel so compelled to know him?

"I . . . don't typically share about my personal life." Odeza's tone indicated that was the end of the conversation.

They sat in silence. The gurgle of the jets and the radio static sound of the tiny foam bubbles popping filled the space between them. Alethia did not feel content letting their conversation end there, especially after feeling responsible for making things weird. Maybe if she shared something personal about herself, he would open up more to her.

"I've always wanted to pack my bags and leave without warning—just take off, go somewhere, anywhere. To explore the world and force myself out of my comfort zone. But I've always been too scared. Scared of the unknown. Scared of not knowing every detail of what to expect. Scared of being disappointed that the adventure wouldn't fill the emptiness. To experience that now, here, so unexpectedly . . . I guess that probably explains why I'm so uptight. I find comfort and safety in being able to control and predict my surroundings." Alethia didn't know why that was what she landed on to share. She looked over to Odeza, the anticipation of his reaction making her stomach flutter.

Odeza's eyes were intently upon her. She felt naked, and it had nothing to do with the fact that most of her body was exposed in a hot tub with an almost stranger. It had everything to do with her vulnerability and the way his eyes were unflinchingly locked onto her. She knew she should look away again, break the intense moment that had her heartbeat quickening. Alethia could feel the buzz of the whiskey egging her on to *not* break the eye contact, to perhaps scoot a little closer to the beautiful man before her.

"My father had a friend who took his life," Odeza said abruptly, "and after that my dad was never right in the head again. He started drinking. I was eleven.

Things changed a lot after that." Odeza spoke the words quiet but evenly. She could have sworn she saw his eyes become shiny, on the brink of tearing up, but his voice didn't waver. He was no longer looking at her. He looked down at the water, obviously absorbed in memory.

"Odeza . . . I . . . I'm so sorry," Alethia said. She moved closer to him, not for the same reason her body had desired moments ago, but because she wanted to comfort him. Did she dare touch him? The thought of placing her hand on top of his felt so natural to Alethia in this moment, but her intuition warned her the touch would mean something more, no matter how innocent she meant it. Alethia shoved a cork into the mouth of her overly cautious, control-freak inner voice and placed her hand on Odeza's arm, which was still draped over the edge of the hot tub.

His eyes shot to her hand instantly, and then slowly dragged up to meet her eyes. Alethia swallowed. She noticed his glance briefly dip to her lips and back up.

Then, without warning, Odeza stood.

"I should go check on the food," he stated and made his way to the house.

Alethia slumped back in her seat. So many emotions flooded her. Disappointment. Relief. Rejection. Confusion.

21. ODEZA
JANUARY 2073

The clock on the wall ticked silently in the background as Odeza stared up at the ceiling in his room at the cabin. He had been awake for over an hour already, just lying there waiting for the sun to come up.

Last night had been . . . odd. After the hot tub, Odeza and Alethia shared very few words. He knew he had been an ass. He had shut her out and been cold. It was bothering him more than he felt it should. He knew what his assignment was. He had been effective thus far in carrying it out, as far as he could tell. But whatever their exchange had been in the hot tub—and how it had affected him—that was definitely not a part of the plan.

There could be no *feelings* involved between him and Alethia. There was no question about that. That would be an utter disaster. So, there he lay, in the silence of the early hours, trying to turn his brain off. Waiting for the day to begin. What an interesting day it would be.

I might as well just get up, Odeza thought. He took a long hot shower and dressed in his suit and tie for the day. He thought of Alethia's words from last night: *"You're a suit and tie guy in my mind."*

Odeza opened the bedroom door to head out to the kitchen and nearly ran into Alethia.

"Oh!" she startled.

Odeza took in her red cheeks, forehead dripping in sweat, the hoodie, leggings, and running shoes she wore.

"What have you been up to?" Odeza quipped, crossing his arms as he leaned against the doorframe. He retreated further into his shell of elusiveness. He needed their dynamic to return to what it had been.

"Running, obviously," she retorted and gestured to her attire. She then brushed past him without another word.

Ouch. Her dismissal of him hurt more than he wanted to admit. She went into her room, closing the door behind her. He heard the shower in her bathroom turn on.

DISSIPATION

Odeza felt anxious. He couldn't remember the last time he felt anxiety like this. He typically kept his emotions as dull as possible. *Stop caring*, he chided himself. *So what if she's pissed at you? What do you care?* Part of Odeza was intrigued by her anger and what it meant—but, once again, he told himself not to be.

* * * *

The car ride to the Allsbrook Village Ascensio site was strained. Alethia still was not speaking to Odeza. They had a long day ahead of them, and Odeza wanted—no, *needed*—this tour to go as planned. Placing the car in park, he turned to look at Alethia.

"I'm sorry," he said with all the sincerity he could muster. She looked at him with her brows furrowed. "I know I was . . . cold to you last night, and you didn't deserve that. You opened up, and I returned the favor by shutting down. I'm not trying to make an excuse for my behavior, but I struggle with my past. I don't know what came over me. As I said last night, I don't really talk about my personal life."

Alethia's brows softened, as did those soulful brown eyes. To his dismay, Odeza's stomach tightened at the sight.

"I can accept that," she said, her tone cautiously neutral. "Let's just . . . forget about it. Now I know not to go there." She broke eye contact and examined the cuff of her jacket.

"Thank you," was the only thing Odeza could think of to respond. He opened his door, and she did too. He noted that she did not wait for him to offer her assistance out of the vehicle, despite how sore he knew she was from their snowboarding escapade.

He continued watching her as they approached the building. This facility was drastically different from the one at SeaPoint Bay. Today, Alethia would see a vastly different piece of the puzzle that was Ascensio, Inc.

They had reached the lobby, and Odeza's cellphone began buzzing. It was Elizabeth.

"I have to take this. I'll be just a sec," Odeza said to Alethia, leaving her to sit in the waiting room and stepping back outside.

"Hello?"

"Dezzy, how good it is to hear your voice," Elizabeth purred.

"Likewise," Odeza responded, matching her tone but rolling his eyes. "Alethia and I just got on site; can I call you back?"

"Is she in earshot?" Elizabeth had lowered her voice.

"No, I stepped outside. Everything good?"

"You tell me, darling. Is everything going *accordingly*?"

No. It honestly wasn't. Odeza felt a knot forming in his stomach.

"I might need more time, Liz," Odeza replied quietly. He looked over his shoulder. Alethia was looking right at him through the window. She raised her eyebrows at him, making a face that seemed to say, "*What's going on?*" He knew she couldn't hear his conversation with Elizabeth, but he also knew this didn't look great.

"Why?" Elizabeth demanded, "What's going on?"

"Look, everything's fine, she's just ... very closed off. I'm having a hard time reading her. But I'm working on it."

"Well, you have a couple days left on your little trip, so I hope you will be calling me with some good news soon." Elizabeth's tone left no room for interpretation; it was a threat. She ended the call before Odeza could respond. He drew in a deep breath and pushed the air back out. Sliding his phone back into his pocket, Odeza went back inside to where Alethia waited for him.

"Is everything alright?" Alethia asked. Her tone was neutral but her eyes analytical.

"Of course." Odeza tossed his head to the side with a coy smile.

22. ALETHIA
JANUARY 2073

Alethia stared out the window of the plane. She wished so badly that it was headed towards home. But, of course, it wasn't. They had one stop left on this cluster of a trip. The last four days had left Alethia reeling.

The Allsbrook Village facility had been a stark contrast from the SeaPoint Bay site. While the patients in SeaPoint were thriving and showing miraculous quality of life with this *treatment* they were testing, the patients at Allsbrook were … not. She saw so many lost and vacant faces. Their recreation room was not filled with joyful participants interacting. There were, however, many people shuffling around or slumped into chairs avoiding eye contact.

It had unnerved her.

Odeza had explained that SeaPoint was the first and only site so far to test their new serum. They were hoping to begin trials in Allsbrook soon.

Alethia grappled with the idea of a serum that miraculously cured ailments of the psyche. It didn't seem possible to her. And was it safe? What would the long-term effects be? Yet . . . it appeared to be working.

And then there was Odeza. She had been more than uncomfortable around him ever since they had a vulnerable moment in the hot tub and then he completely iced her out. He had resumed his nonchalant and flippant façade, acting as if nothing occurred.

Was it a façade? Alethia felt that she had glimpsed moments of what she wondered was his true self underneath his cocky demeanor. A gentler, caring, and thoughtful man. But it didn't matter. He had clearly drawn the line, and they were not to get to know each other on a deeper level.

It suited Alethia just fine. At least that's what she kept telling herself—they didn't need to have a relationship beyond supervisor-subordinate. She just wished her body would follow suit with this decision. But every time she was near him, she had such a keen sense of his closeness. The air had energy. She was filled with anticipation. When she looked too long into his eyes or at his body ... No.

She couldn't go there. There was still the sting of rejection flowing through her from his immediate exit from the hot tub when she had done nothing other than lightly touch him on the arm. The door was closed. There shouldn't even *be* a door.

Luckily, they didn't have seats together for this flight. Odeza was seated a few rows behind her. She had spent the entire flight so far ruminating on everything and wanting to be somewhere else.

"Ladies and gentlemen, it is a bright and sunny eighty-two degrees in Fort Kenzington, 11:05 local time. Please remain seated and make sure your seatbelts are fastened. We are approximately twenty minutes from landing at Kenzington International Airport. Flight attendants, please prepare for decent," the pilot's muffled voice announced over the intercom.

As the plane began its decent from the sky and the ground below came closer into view, Alethia scoped out the city. Just like the other two destinations, she had never been to Fort Kenzington, though she had heard of it. Back in the desert of District 8, they weren't far from home at all. Desert View was likely a half day's car ride away.

Fort Kenzington was a large metropolis. She could see skyscrapers in the distance and a sprawling maze of suburban areas that flanked the urban inner city. She could also spot the familiar sandy mountain ranges far on the horizon. They flew over lime green foliage and cacti that dotted the landscape and disappeared as they got closer to the city.

* * * *

Alethia and Odeza made their way through the airport and car rental center surprisingly quickly. Alethia sat in the passenger seat while Odeza drove to their next destination.

"We won't be touring the last facility until tomorrow," Odeza said casually as he drove and kept his eyes fixed on the road ahead.

Great. Alethia thought. "And what escapade do you have planned for us in the meantime?" she bit out, not bothering to hide her annoyance any longer.

DISSIPATION

At her remark, Odeza turned his head towards her, raising his eyebrows. "Would you prefer we went straight to the hotel and sat around staring each other down for the remainder of the day?" Odeza shot back evenly.

Alethia's mouth dropped open. She wasn't expecting him to bite back at her. She was the one who deserved to be annoyed. Not him. What had she ever done but go along with his stupid plans this whole week and try to get to know him better? Anger rose to the surface inside Alethia's chest. She suddenly felt as if the car were sweltering despite the air conditioning. She narrowed her eyes at him.

"Perhaps we should," she retorted.

"Well, then, it's settled," he obliged.

Alethia crossed her arms and looked out the window. At least if they went to the hotel, she could be alone in her room.

Odeza kept to his word and drove straight to the hotel. It didn't take them long to get there. Alethia felt relieved to get out of the car and get a little air.

Despite their harsh exchange in the car, Odeza still pulled Alethia's luggage out of the trunk for her and opened the lobby door for her. She begrudgingly muttered thanks.

The hotel they were staying at had all the bells and whistles of their previous lodgings. The lobby was gorgeous, with sparkling marble floors, floor-to-ceiling windows offering views of the city park across the street, and a crystalline chandelier hanging above a gurgling water fountain in the middle of the open space.

A young woman with black hair and leopard print glasses stood behind the check-in counter. She welcomed them with a dazzling smile. Odeza told her there was a reservation under his name. She quickly typed away on her keyboard, took Odeza's company credit card, and continued clicking about with her long, manicured nails as she explained all the amenities.

"Here's your card back, Mr. Speer. You will be staying in room 516. It's always a pleasure to do business with Ascensio, and we hope you enjoy your stay. Please let me know if you need anything at all," she cooed as she handed them two key cards.

Odeza frowned as he took the key cards. "Room 516, and . . . ?"

"Is there a problem with that room, sir?" the woman asked.

"There should be two separate rooms. My colleague and I are both staying here tonight," he explained, irritated, as he motioned towards Alethia.

"Ah, *so* sorry about that, sir!" she began frantically clicking and typing on her computer. "There must have been some mistake. Let me look into this for you."

They waited as the furrow in the receptionists' brow began to deepen.

"Mr. Speer, there is only one room booked on this reservation. I'm so sorry, but . . . I don't have another room for you," she expressed, her voice strained, and her eyes bugged out. "Normally I would be able to add another room, but we are completely booked with the festival of lights that's in town . . . I'm sure all the hotels in the area are."

Odeza ran a hand over his face and through his hair.

"Okay. Just . . . Give me one moment," he said to the receptionist, then turned toward Alethia. "I don't know how this happened. Let me make some calls. There's no way *every hotel in the city* is booked."

Alethia nodded at Odeza and gave the receptionist a reassuring smile. The poor woman looked as if she feared for her job because of this one error.

Figuring she should make herself useful, Alethia also pulled out her phone and began searching for other hotels. They both looked for what seemed like forever. As it turned out, all the hotels in the area were indeed full. Fort Kenzington was a large city, and the closest place with more than one room available was an hour away . . . and it was a two-star motel. From the pictures on the internet, it looked like one could easily be murdered there, or perhaps contract an infectious disease of some kind.

Alethia met Odeza's exasperated expression.

"What do you want to do?" Odeza asked her. The angst from earlier had left his tone. He now sounded . . . almost defeated.

"It doesn't seem like we have a whole lot of options," Alethia replied. His shift in demeanor had softened her tone as well. She felt a pang of empathy for his exasperation, then reminded herself to keep her guard up.

"Does that mean you want to stay here?" he asked slowly.

"Well, I don't think either one of us *wants* to be in this situation, but like I said, we don't really have another feasible option."

"Alright then," Odeza said and then frowned. "I'll of course take the couch or cot or chair ... or *floor*, if need be."

Alethia's stomach clenched at the thought of the two of them sharing a bedroom. She didn't think it mattered if he slept in the bathtub—she probably wasn't going to sleep at all tonight.

After assuring the frantic receptionist that everything was fine, Alethia and Odeza made their way to the elevator. Alone inside, they both fidgeted—Odeza with the case of his phone, finding some reason to pop the phone in and out of the case, and Alethia with her shirt sleeve, locating every strand of lint that could be found and plucking it off. The elevator ride felt to have been an hour long by the time they arrived at their floor.

Odeza motioned for Alethia to exit first. She stepped ahead of him and headed down the hallway. When she stopped in front of room 516, he reached over her and unlocked the door with the key card.

They stepped into the room and stopped. Both their eyes went straight to the singular king-sized bed right in front of them.

23. ODEZA
JANUARY 2073

Odeza glanced briefly at Alethia before ducking his head and going over to place his bag down by the little seating area in their room. There was, in fact, a couch, thank goodness. Alethia looked tight as a bow string.

Odeza couldn't imagine a more awkward situation, especially when he was trying to keep things professional with Alethia after their tense last few days. He had no idea why she had lashed out in the car. She seemed pissed at him still. He knew he had pushed her away when she had tried to be kind, but he didn't understand why she was still fuming.

Odeza pretended to go through his bag. From the corner of his eye, he watched Alethia place her suitcase on the bed and start doing the same. They needed to get out of this room. His idea of sitting and staring each other down had never been a serious one, of course, but *this* was painful.

"Under the circumstances, if you are perhaps now interested, my original idea for the afternoon was to go on a hike. I promise it won't be strenuous like the snowboarding . . . and the hike has great views of the surrounding area," Odeza offered, praying she would agree.

"Are you implying I can't handle strenuous activities?" Alethia asked in a tone that danced on the line of being almost playful. "Because I recall handling the '*strenuous*' snowboarding *quite well*." She raised an eyebrow at him, the smallest smile playing at the corners of her mouth.

Odeza returned the cocked brow and smirked at her.

"I think what you mean to say," Alethia continued coyly, "is that your idea of sitting and staring each other down was *awful* and you would suggest anything to get us out of this room."

Was this merely her way of lightening the mood of their precarious situation? Or had she finally forgiven him and moved past whatever had angered her? Either way, he had to admit she was one hundred percent correct.

"Your intuition is top-notch," he returned.

* * * *

The trail was about thirty minutes outside the city. It began with foothills covered in towering blooming cacti. Various sage brush and other types of desert foliage contrasted brightly against the dusty ground. The weather was impeccable, a sunny eighty degrees with a caressing breeze. Soon, the trail would begin to ascend into steeper terrain. Odeza had been on this hike before, and he knew the summit would display views of the city on one side and the surrounding peaks on the other.

The atmosphere between Alethia and Odeza had become more easy-going since their banter in the hotel room. Since the day they'd met, Alethia had never been particularly talkative or warm towards him. So Odeza supposed this was their 'normal'.

There was a pull in his chest to know her in a deeper way, even though his head told him that would be a disaster. Her mind intrigued him. She seemed to analyze situations so keenly and was aware of nearly *everything* around her. Intelligence was highly attractive to Odeza. Not only that, but she could keep up with his arrogant ass. She wasn't afraid to put him in his place. While it threw him, it also . . . turned him on a little.

The path had narrowed, and Alethia took the lead. Odeza had to make a conscious effort to turn his attention away from her and to, well, *anything* else. The leggings, sports bra, and tank top she wore left just enough to the imagination. Her toned muscles and elegant figure made it clear that she worked out. The sun made her golden hair glisten as her ponytail swayed to the rhythm of her walking.

"Why are you being so quiet?" Alethia asked, yanking Odeza from his observations.

"I guess I was just thinking," he replied honestly.

"Care to share what about? Or is that too *personal*?"

Odeza sighed. He supposed that was a fair remark.

"I was honestly thinking about you," he said, to his own astonishment. *Idiot*, he scolded himself.

Alethia stopped in her tracks and turned to look at him. Her cheeks were pink from hiking in the warm sun, and a trickle of sweat trailed down her temple. She was breathing slightly harder than normal.

"What about me?" she asked, furrowing her brow.

"Well, just about our trip. How things got weird. I wish they hadn't. I . . . regret how I treated you. And I wish you'd tell me what you're upset about, because I don't like feeling like I hurt you," Odeza answered honestly again. Damn her. Why was this woman able to crack his defenses so easily?

"What I'm upset about is exactly what you just said," she answered incredulously. "You just play games, Odeza, and it's annoying. I wish *you* would just be real, like you were in the hot tub for the *one second* before *you* made things weird. Maybe you should tell me what *that* was all about," she fumed. With that, Alethia turned around and began walking again.

Odeza was stunned. This whole "honest feelings" thing was a slippery slope. He followed her.

"Well, I . . . " he began, then trailed off. Odeza was in such uncharted territory. Should he continue being honest, or not? Everything in his heart wanted to be honest with her. To see those big brown eyes look upon him with something other than disdain. He wanted her to like him. In a cordial way, of course, he lied to himself.

"I feel like I explained that already in the car the other day when I apologized. I just don't know how to get to know someone on a personal level. I don't like putting myself out there," he confessed.

"I get that," Alethia replied as she kept walking ahead of him. "But why? What have I done to make you feel so uncomfortable around me that you can't trust me? I feel like you're two different people. Some moments, I feel like I see the real you . . . but most times you just come off as, well, phony, if I'm being honest." She huffed her words as her breathing became heavier in the thinning air. They were approaching the summit.

"I didn't realize you thought I was phony," he said, a little hurt. "But what about you, though? You keep all your cards close to your chest. You're not much more expressive than I am," he argued, taking deeper breaths himself as they hiked upward.

"*Okay*, maybe phony wasn't the right word. I don't know, Odeza . . . I just feel like you hide yourself and pretend like nothing in the world fazes you when it actually does. And I may keep a lot to myself, but at least I don't act like an entirely different person when I'm *'keeping my cards close to my chest,'*" she emphasized, using air quotes.

"But I don't understand why that would even bother you," Odeza countered. "You usually don't seem to want anything to do with me regardless."

"And you don't seem to care one way or another if I do," Alethia protested. She again stopped abruptly to turn around and face him. Standing on a steeper incline ahead, and she was nearly at eye level with him. Odeza, taken aback by her sudden halt, had to quickly step back to keep from running into her.

For the first time, she appeared wild, her usual perfection and composure replaced by a stark, ruffled contrast. Her eyes blazed into his, her chest heaving as she tried to catch her breath. She had placed her hands on her hips and was unflinchingly staring at him. Whatever response Odeza had been prepared to fire back fell from his mind. Odeza stared back at her. She was so beautiful. He took her rage for passion, and it overwhelmed him.

He didn't know what his face was confessing, but whatever Alethia saw in it softened her edge. She seemed to be scanning his features. Searching for something. Those eyes of hers completely disarmed him. He wanted her to always look at him like this. He didn't want to hurt her. Rile her, absolutely. Get under her skin, yes. But hurt her, never.

24. ALETHIA
JANUARY 2073

Alethia was perplexed. Odeza's eyes shone with emotion. This moment, this exchange—the glimpse of hidden parts of him, the yearning in his eyes—this was what Alethia had been craving since she had touched his arm that night, just before he'd pulled away.

What was happening? Alethia felt the lines being blurred between them. The pull towards him that she felt was taking over her body. She knew she had to regain control of herself so that she didn't act on these wild impulses.

Eyes still locked, Odeza spoke softly. "We're almost at the summit."

Right. The hike. She nodded and turned away from him. But as she moved, Odeza gently placed his hand on her shoulder. She looked back at him.

"Thank you for your honesty," he said.

All Alethia could focus on was his touch. She hated that she loved it. She wanted more of it. But he took it away just as quickly as he'd given it.

"You're welcome," she murmured.

They began walking again. It was silent, but this was a very different silence than the beginning of their hike.

As it turned out, Odeza had been right, the summit was only about fifty more feet from where they'd been.

It was beautiful. The afternoon sun beat down on the distant city, glinting off the glass skyscrapers. All the other buildings were mere colored dots. The desert plain on the far side of the city stretched on to infinity. Alethia turned to take in the rest of the view and sucked in a breath.

Now that *is beautiful*, she thought.

Magnificent orange rock, some smooth, some jagged from erosion, dominated the landscape. The green cacti and bright blue sky framed the orange canvas perfectly.

Alethia turned towards Odeza.

He wasn't looking at the view at all—he was looking at her. As if embarrassed to be caught, he placed his hands in the pocket of his shorts and looked towards the city.

"I'm glad I got to see this," Alethia said. "Thank you."

"Of course," Odeza replied, keeping his eyes on the view.

She walked over to him and gazed at the maze of buildings.

"Can you point out where the Ascensio facility is from here?" she asked.

"It's there." He pointed towards the outskirts of Fort Kenzington to the largest structure in that section of the city. It looked like a big cement box.

"Oh," Alethia said, frowning. "It looks . . . A little dismal from here, if I'm being honest." She was accustomed to the elegant structures with plenty of windows and art. This building could be mistaken for a prison from this view.

"Well, I've been meaning to bring up our tour tomorrow. It will be . . . a little different than the other two," he said, his tone turning serious and his posture tightening. "Fort Kenzington, as you may know, is home to one of the nation's largest maximum-security prisons. A lot of our referrals for this facility come from psych evals that are conducted there. The Ascensio facility at Fort Kenzington is home to many violent offenders."

"Oh . . . " she responded. So, it *was* like a prison. "What will the tour entail tomorrow?"

"Essentially, you will meet with a few of the patients, but in a very . . . *structured* way. There will be limited access to the different wings again, for safety purposes."

Alethia pondered, unsure of what to say. Odeza almost seemed to be insinuating she might be frightened to go. But it honestly didn't intimidate or scare her to visit the facility. "I'm fine with that, Odeza," she assured him. "I can handle visiting with a few offenders."

Odeza turned to face her. The second their eyes locked, she felt that pulling sensation in her gut. He seemed to be appraising her. Then, he cocked his head to the side gave her an amused smile.

DISSIPATION

"I don't doubt it," he said.

* * * *

By the time they made it back down the mountain it was early evening, and they were starving. They grabbed fast food hamburgers and drove back to the inner city where they were staying. It had been a long day with the traveling and the hiking, and neither one of them had known what else they felt like doing, so they returned to the hotel. The sun was setting as they arrived.

Odeza had been correct, the hike had not really been *that* strenuous. However, Alethia's body was still recovering from the snowboarding fall, and each step she took pained her. She had to muster every ounce of self-preservation to walk normally as they approached their room. Her shoulders were a ball of knots from the stress of the past few days, her back was still pinched from the wipeout she'd taken on the mountain, and her hamstrings and calves were extremely tight, which didn't help her back.

Odeza pulled the keycard out and opened the door to their room. He gestured for her to enter first. Alethia went into the room and sat on the bed. Odeza closed the door behind them and walked to the window, adjusting the semi-transparent curtain so he could peer at the park below.

Alethia felt a headache escalating into a migraine, a consequence of her tense muscles. She closed her eyes, gently rubbing her thumb and index finger in circles over her lids.

"Are you alright?" Odeza asked, having turned back towards her.

"Oh yeah, I'm fine. Just a little headache," she downplayed, not wanting to look like a baby.

"Can I get you some water?" Odeza offered.

"That would be great, thank you," she replied, giving him a soft smile.

Odeza went to the sink and filled a glass. He rummaged in his bag for a moment before pulling out a small pill bottle.

"I have some ibuprofen if you want some," he said, holding up the pills.

Alethia accepted the pain medicine and water. She knew the pain wouldn't subside as long as the muscles in her shoulders stayed taut. She began pressing her fingers down and making small circles on her shoulders to ease the tightness.

"Tension headache?" Odeza asked. He sat on the bed beside her, a respectable distance away.

"Mmhmm," she confirmed, closing her eyes as she continued trying to work her knots out.

"I know how those feel, I get them too," Odeza sympathized. "You want some help with that?" he asked, nodding at her attempts to massage herself.

Alethia's eyes flew open. Did Odeza just offer to give her a massage? She should say no. She should definitely say no.

Right?

Alethia thought of how it felt earlier today when he'd gently touched her on the shoulder. She'd wanted more of his touch. She still did. But she knew she shouldn't. It would be completely inappropriate to accept a massage from him in the single hotel room they had to share... wouldn't it?

"Really?" she asked him, despite herself.

"If you'd like me to," he ventured. His eyes seemed to dance. There was a strange emotion on his face that Alethia couldn't quite pin.

"Well, alright," she acquiesced, giving in to the temptation of his touch.

Still sitting, she turned to face the headboard. Her heart began to pound, and she felt her cheeks flush in anticipation.

He brushed her long ponytail over her left shoulder with the path of his fingertips leaving an electric buzz on her skin. Odeza placed his hands on her shoulders and pushed his thumbs in rhythmic circles over the knots, causing heavenly release. She felt as if his touch would melt her into a puddle right there on the bed. She closed her eyes and leaned her head back slightly, savoring it.

With his close proximity, Alethia could hear Odeza's breath going in and out of his nose.

Was his breathing quicker than normal?

It certainly seemed so. Alethia wanted so badly to know if she affected him the way he was affecting her. But she couldn't go there. Despite the lines they were blurring, Odeza had freaked out the last time she'd tried to get closer to him. She would not put herself out there like that again. Nor should she. For goodness' sake, they worked together. He was her *superior*. Not to mention she knew so very little about him.

DISSIPATION

Odeza started working his thumbs farther down underneath her shoulder blades. A contented sigh escaped her, and she felt him press harder into her back. She could not help but lean into the pressure he was applying.

He continued his movements, dragging his thumbs up and down either side of her spine, his fingers now lightly encasing her lower ribs. She arched her back, biting her lip to keep herself from groaning. The relief he was giving her back was divine, but the heat he was otherwise causing her... she should stop this. She was going to do something she regretted.

His thumbs moved even further down her spinal column. With perfect pressure he swept both thumbs across the plain of her lower back. Alethia gasped and tightly squeezed the duvet they sat on.

He paused his hands where they were.

"Too hard?" he whispered, his voice like gravel.

25. ODEZA

JANUARY 2073

Odeza glanced to where Alethia was gripping the duvet. She slowly turned her head to look at him over her shoulder. One look at those burning brown eyes filled with longing completely did him in. Consequences be damned—he needed her. He needed to know how her lips tasted, to hold her close to him, to drive her wildly out of her always-controlled shell.

His hands were still frozen on her lower back. He slightly adjusted them to grip her waist, watching her eyes spark. He leaned towards her, scanning her face for approval. Her chest rose and fell heavily. She glanced down at his lips and back up into his eyes.

DISSIPATION

He could die happily drowning in those piercing irises. He inched closer until he could feel her breath caress his face.

Then, Odeza's phone rang.

The sound shocked the two of them, breaking their enticement. Odeza got up from the bed, pulling his phone from his pocket.

It was Elizabeth, of course, damn her. Answering, he kept his eyes on Alethia. She had broken eye contact and was getting up from the bed.

"Hello?" Odeza groused, trying and failing to mask his frustration. He watched Alethia walk into the bathroom and close the door behind her.

"What's wrong?" Elizabeth demanded.

Odeza closed his eyes and rubbed his lids, trying to regain his faculties. He cleared his throat.

"Nothing is wrong. I'm just tired," he lied.

"No, you sound upset. What's going on?" she pestered.

Odeza took a deep breath. "I couldn't be better, darling, truly. I just miss you, of course," he lied further, attempting to throw her off his trail.

There was a pause on the other end of the line.

"Well, obviously," Elizabeth swooned.

"What's good at corporate?" he inquired, hoping to distract her.

"Oh, the usual, Dezzy, but you know I didn't call you to talk about how things are going with *me*. Though you're such a *sweetheart* to ask," she purred.

Odeza hung his head. He needed to come up with news that would satisfy her. He glanced at the bathroom door. Alethia was still in there, but he needed this conversation to be private. He grabbed the key card from the coffee table and stepped into the hallway.

"Things are going much better from when we last spoke," he said, which was actually not a lie at all from his perspective, though it certainly was within the context of their last conversation.

"Okay . . . details," Elizabeth commanded.

"The last tour really made an impression on Alethia. I think she's coming along exactly as we'd hoped. Of course, we still have one more tour tomorrow, which should solidify her loyalty even further." Odeza's head was spinning with the lies he was telling. He genuinely had no clue what Alethia thought about their facilities, she was so frustratingly quiet the last few days.

DISSIPATION

"Excellent," Elizabeth cooed, her voice dripping with the expectation that he would deliver.

26. ALETHIA
JANUARY 2073

Alethia gripped the bathroom vanity and stared at herself in the mirror. Her cheeks were still burning, but now so were her eyes. She willed them not to dampen.

Someone had called Odeza right in the middle of their . . . whatever the hell that was. She had heard him call whoever it was *darling* in a tone that could not be mistaken for anything other than flirtatious.

Damn him.

It was all just games with him. She knew he was about to kiss her. She would have let him. Dammit, she had *wanted* him to. But saved by the phone call of whoever his *darling* was, nothing happened. Thank goodness nothing did.

DISSIPATION

Alethia was sick to her stomach. He was playing her. And playing whoever was on the other end of the phone, apparently. She could break something she felt so angry and hurt.

And for what? She mocked herself. *How could you be so stupid? You knew better.*

She wanted to go home. She was so done with this stupid trip. But she couldn't leave. Not without risking her job. But did she care? Was it really worth it at this point?

She thought about the patients she desired to help. This potential miracle serum she had so many questions about. How hard she had worked to get her degree and this position. How much she had grown into it over the last several months. She had been feeling so confident and satisfied before leaving on this trip. Before whatever it was that had sparked between her and Odeza.

Well, that spark was out now. Cold and dead.

Still staring herself down in the mirror, Alethia made herself a promise. She was not going to let this man screw her over and take from her what she had worked so hard for.

She was going to stuff everything she'd felt for him and all the betrayal that now pulsed inside her chest into a nice little box inside herself and lock it up.

She would act as if nothing had ever occurred. She would be cordial and distance herself physically and emotionally so he could not hurt her.

And after this trip, she would cease to speak to him unless absolutely necessary.

She heard the hallway door open and close. After collecting herself and wiping emotion from her face, she exited the bathroom. Odeza had gone out into the hallway. Good. She did not wish to have any further interaction with him.

Alethia put her headphones on and climbed into bed, pulling the covers up and facing away from the door. When Odeza eventually returned to the room, she closed her eyes and pretended to sleep.

* * * *

The Ascensio facility at Fort Kenzington had several security checkpoints within its concrete interior. Unlike the other facilities Alethia had visited, which veiled the human suffering ever so slightly with whimsical décor, this facility didn't bother. All of the employees showed no discernable emotion and were posted about like guards. The whole thing put Alethia on edge. She wanted to be back in the warmth of daylight as soon as possible.

Odeza seemed to be walking annoyingly close to her as they were shown to the "visitor's room," which could have fooled Alethia as being an interrogation room at a police station. They had not discussed what happened last night, and their communication this morning had been limited to short, empty pleasantries.

The name of their escort was Dante. He was a good foot taller than Alethia, the same height as Odeza but probably twenty to thirty pounds heavier, all muscle. He had cropped black hair and a neatly trimmed beard. His eyes were dark and intense. He spoke minimally and let no emotion enter his expressions. Alethia took note of a few scars on his arms and one just above his left brow.

"You may sit here," Dante said, gesturing to two metal chairs that sat on one side of a metal table. "I will be bringing in Patient 918. He will enter with restrictive cuffs which will remain on for the duration of the visit for your safety."

Alethia sat down, trying her best to look calm and unfazed. She believed that people were neither good nor bad inherently; it was merely that good and bad things happened to them, and they made good and bad choices. She was not in the business of judging others for what had befallen them or their past actions. She just wanted to help however she could. It didn't settle right with her that this basically mimicked a prison when it was supposed to be a mental health facility.

Odeza sat next to her, angling his body slightly so that it was between her and the door where the patient would enter. Alethia fought to not roll her eyes. If he wanted to be heroic or chivalrous, he could stop making her believe he felt things for her when he clearly did not.

Dante crossed the room and unlocked a heavy metal door. There were two other—employees? Guards? Alethia didn't know what to think of them as they entered, each holding one arm of a man in a grey jumpsuit. His wrists were in handcuffs, as were his ankles. He had just enough chain link to walk. They sat him down in his own metal chair across the room from them.

The man's black eyes were glued to Alethia from the moment the door had opened. They devoured her as though she were something he could consume. He smiled at her with an unsightly grin that completely unnerved her.

Odeza's eyes were locked on the man. He had shifted in his seat again, so the angle of his body remained slightly between her and the man. His muscles were tense, as if he was prepared to spring from his seat at the slightest threat.

The room was silent. Alethia suddenly recalled that the purpose of this visit was for her to meet patients and talk to them about their experiences. They were waiting on her to speak. Alethia cleared her throat, and the man's eyes lit up with glee at the sight of her obvious discomfort.

"Hello," Alethia offered in her best attempt at sounding normal. It did not sound normal. She sounded like a sheep among wolves.

"Hi there, beautiful," The man crooned, his eyes taking in every inch of her body.

From the corner of her eye, Alethia saw Odeza's jaw tighten.

"You can call me Ms. Burkshire. And your name?"

"My name? You can call me whatever you want to, sweetheart—oh, sorry, I mean *Ms.* Burkshire. Does that mean you're available?" he cackled.

"Knock it off, 918," one of the guards beside him warned.

"*Better be a good boy or you'll get the stick*," Patient 918 whispered to himself maniacally, making the hair on Alethia's arms raise.

"The stick?" Alethia questioned, her eyebrows raising. He didn't mean they beat him in here, did he?

"He's not talking about us," Dante interjected. "He has a history of physical abuse as a child."

Patient 918's eyes shot to Dante. He spat on the floor. "Mmm, yes, don't *you* know everything," he said, glaring daggers.

"If you don't mind me asking, why are you here?" Alethia asked, figuring she may as well get to the point if it meant getting out of the room quicker.

"Hm, let me think," Patient 918 said, the pitch of his voice going up in mock sweetness. "Probably because I killed my mother . . . oh, and my father . . . and, how could I forget, my brothers and sisters, too." He counted his crimes on his fingertips as he rattled them off. His eyes flashed back to Alethia. He stared her down without blinking. "When the cops showed up, I was playing in a pool of their blood, laughing. Oh, I was nine, by the way," he added, as if it were a minimal detail. "Hence the reason I'm in a psychiatric facility and not prison. Been here ever since."

"Why did you do it?" Alethia asked calmly.

"Because they deserved it," he said through gritted teeth. He spit on the floor again.

"They hurt you," Alethia said softly.

"Oh, do you feel sorry for me?" The man purred, "Why don't you come sit on my lap and cheer me up? You can feel how *happy* I am to see you." He began to drag his hand up the leg of his pants.

"That's *enough*," Odeza declared, standing up in front of Alethia, blocking her from the man's view. "We're done here," he said to Dante.

The guards hoisted Patient 918 up by his arms and escorted him out the door he'd entered from. Dante then unlocked the door for Alethia and Odeza to exit.

Odeza told her their tour was over, and they left the facility.

27. ALETHIA
JANUARY 2073

Odeza gripped the steering wheel with white knuckles. His eyes bore into the road ahead as he worked his jaw silently.

"I hope you didn't end the tour on my account," Alethia said. "I was fine, you know."

Odeza turned his head and made eye contact with her. There was so much tension in his features that Alethia wondered if he was going to yell at her. She was surprised when he did the opposite as he looked back toward the road.

"It wasn't you I was worried about," he said so quietly she barely heard him over the hum of the highway as they raced on.

"He couldn't do anything, he was chained up," Alethia replied.

"I wasn't worried about him, either, Alethia," Odeza emphasized each word in a controlled tone.

"Okay . . . then what was the issue?" Alethia pried. The whole point of this trip was for her to see these facilities, and she'd barely gotten a glimpse of this one after Odeza made them leave in haste.

Odeza let out a sigh, briefly closing his eyes before staring ahead as he drove. He rolled his shoulders but kept that iron grip on the wheel.

"What is going on with you?" Alethia asked, wondering if she should be the one behind the wheel.

"I need a drink," he ground out and suddenly veered toward the nearest exit.

They sat in silence as Odeza sped down the streets until he found a bar. Alethia had to almost jog to keep up with him as he strode inside and asked the waitress for a table in the back.

If Alethia could ride the waves of Odeza's moods and not fall out of the boat, she would consider herself a master sailor. But it was a bit too much for her to handle, so she told Odeza she needed a moment. He followed the hostess to a booth in the back as Alethia made her way to use the ladies' room.

On her way back, she noticed a man with shaggy brown hair and a worn leather jacket sitting at a booth alone. His brown eyes were bloodshot, and it looked like he'd been crying. He couldn't be much older than her. Her heart ached at the sight of his brokenness.

"Are you okay?" she asked softly, hoping it wasn't an unwelcome intrusion.

Watery eyes met hers and he huffed out a breath. "I'm fine," he said with the cracked voice of someone who has indeed been crying. He raised up his glass and added, "I've just been dumped." He offered her a half-hearted smile and downed the last of his drink.

"I'm sorry," she condoled, offering him a sympathetic smile in return. *Poor sap*, she thought as she continued past him.

She plopped down in the cushioned leather seat across from Odeza in the dim and cozy section of the bar he had chosen. Soft jazz played in the background. It being the middle of the day, they were one of the very few people there. A tall, slim woman with her hair slicked back in a bun came and asked them what they wanted to drink.

"Surprise me," Odeza cajoled, "but make it strong."

The waitress raised her eyebrows and then looked to Alethia.

"I'll have whatever he's having," she said with a chagrined smile.

Once the waitress walked away, Alethia met Odeza's waiting gaze. She shot him an expression that said, *What the hell is going on and why are we day drinking?*

"I was worried I was going to punch that asshole in the face," Odeza growled under his breath. "And anyone else in that place that so much as looked at you wrong. *That* is why we had to leave. And why I need a drink."

Alethia's spine tingled at the utter possession in his tone. Her stomach clenched and heart quickened. She quickly shut the door on her reaction to him as she reminded herself she was not the only one he was *possessing*. Her emotion quickly turned to annoyance.

"Who called you last night?" she blurted and immediately regretted doing so.

"What?" Odeza asked, puzzled.

"The phone call? The one you had to step out to take? To your *darling*?" Alethia attempted to sound like she was teasing him, like it didn't make a difference to her. She was horrified at herself for bringing this up.

She watched Odeza's face. The furrow of his brow slowly relaxed as something seemed to click for him.

"Is that why you've been giving me the cold shoulder this morning?" Odeza challenged, his eyes suddenly dazzling her with a playful shine.

"I haven't been giving—hey, don't turn this around on me. I asked you a question first," Alethia shot back, crossing her arms.

Odeza sucked in air between his teeth dramatically and flicked his eyebrows up. "Testy," he whispered as the waitress approached with their drinks.

Odeza's eyes did not leave Alethia's while the woman sat down two short glasses with amber liquid. Before she could walk away, his eyes remaining glued to Alethia's, he downed his drink in one swig and passed his glass back to the waitress. "I'll have another," he said.

Alethia's heart pounded at the way Odeza's eyes seemed to see straight past any barrier she set up. It was impossible to figure out which version of him she was going to get. She hated the damn butterflies that pinged around in her stomach at the attention he was giving her. But it wasn't right. Not if he had a "darling."

"I need some air," Alethia breathed and abruptly got up from the table, making a beeline for the exit.

"Alethia, come back," he called.

She ignored him and made her way outside. She had no plan and no idea where she would go, but she kept walking. The fresh air helped to clear her head.

Odeza followed after her.

"Alethia, wait. Will you please let me explain? I get it, I've acted completely erratically today."

You don't say? Alethia rolled her eyes and kept walking.

"Elizabeth," Odeza called, "As in Elizabeth Straumen, my *boss*. That's who called me. She's the farthest thing from *my darling*, Alethia. It's a stupid pet name I call her when I'm trying to get her off my case and she's delirious enough to fall for it."

She stopped.

Odeza jogged to close the remaining distance between them but stopped a few feet away, still behind her.

Alethia continued gazing up the desolate street at the claustrophobic city buildings. Odeza waited for a response behind her. Alethia took a few deep breaths and counted to ten in her mind to compose herself before turning around.

"I see." It was all Alethia could think to say. Part of her felt excited by this news. Perhaps he wasn't trying to screw her over after all. But what was she supposed to say? What did she want to say? Words failed her.

They stood there watching each other. If felt as if they were in a small box together, unable to escape the others' presence.

Odeza cleared his throat and adjusted the sleeves of his shirt.

"So, anyways," he began, suddenly giving Alethia the impression he felt self-conscious, "I apologize for my behavior today, and if yesterday you had the impression that I was . . . seeing someone else. I'm not. Um . . . " He trailed off, tripping over his words.

Alethia shook her head and sighed. "You are so confusing."

He frowned. "Sorry?"

"I just . . . never know which version of you I'm going to get," Alethia admitted. She kicked a pebble that was under her foot and fidgeted with the bracelet she wore.

"What version do you like the best?" he asked.

Alethia looked up. "Well, I prefer when people are genuine and don't try to hide who they are," she challenged.

Odeza crossed his arms. "Really?" he mused.

"*Yes.*"

He narrowed his eyes slightly. "I find that statement a little ironic coming from you, Burkshire." His tone danced between playful and hurt by what she'd said.

"Why is that?"

"Because you hide all the time."

His words may as well have slapped her across the face. She stepped towards him, heat rising to her face.

"I do not hide," she snapped.

"Oh, don't you?" Odeza stepped towards her and tilted his head to the side. "You don't ever pretend like things don't faze you when they actually do?" He took another step. "Like you aren't afraid, even when you are?"

One more step. They were mere inches from each other now. "Like you don't *feel* things when you do?"

He was close enough that Alethia could smell the teakwood and spice cologne he wore. She glared up at him, wanting to look strong, wanting to look . . . unfazed. Damn it, he was right. He was completely right about her. She did hide. She hid all the time from her feelings and fears and tried to present perfection, always.

But she was not perfect.

She could never be.

Her face fell as the weight of the conversation pressed on her. She felt naked before him. She lowered her head, not wanting to be seen.

"Alethia." Odeza's voice was silken as he lifted her chin with his index finger until their eyes met again. The look he gave her made her entire body hum with warm electricity.

"I see you," he said. "Even when you try to hide, I see you. And you are worthy."

Tears stung Alethia's eyes as she tried to blink them away. These words went deep into the inner places of her soul causing a sort of healing. She'd had no idea how much she needed to hear that. She closed her eyes; a tear escaped and ran down her cheek.

Odeza moved the hand that was under her chin to cup her cheek and brush the tear away with his thumb. His hand was warm, and she leaned into his touch, savoring it. She opened her eyes to find him staring, eyes full of longing and desire. She slowly brought her hand up to his face and laid it against his cheek, matching the one on her own.

Odeza leaned down until their faces were inches from each other. He seemed to search her face looking for any sign of dissent. She quirked up the side of her lips in a knowing smile, an invitation.

At that, Odeza wrapped his free hand around her waist and pulled her into him. He pressed his lips to hers. His kiss seemed to convey all his angst and sadness, heaviness and excitement, playfulness and longing. Everything she had come to know as the ways that he expressed himself.

Alethia brought her hands to his face and kissed him back intently.

They broke apart just long enough to look at each other and Alethia found him smiling. It was a smile she'd never seen on him, and it made her heart leap. The skin around his eyes crinkled in an endearing manner as his straight white teeth flashed. She wanted to see it on him again and again. She smiled back.

But as soon as his smile appeared, it was gone. A look of fear came over Odeza's face and he straightened.

"We need to go," he said to her. "There are some things I need to tell you."

28. ALETHIA
JANUARY 2073

Odeza drove them back to the hotel. The car ride was a mixture of sexual tension and apprehension. Alethia was frustrated again by Odeza's sudden silence. When they finally got to the hotel, he pulled into a parking space in the parking garage. Odeza leaned over and brushed her hair behind her ear, sending bolts of electricity down her spine. He put his lips so close to her ear they almost touched.

"Leave your phone in the car," he whispered. He then slid his own phone out of his pocket and put it in the glove compartment, leaving it open for her to do the same.

She was about to object when he placed his index finger gently on her lips and shook his head. His eyes were full of warning. Alethia obeyed him, and they got out of the car. She threw him a quizzical look, but he merely placed his hand on her lower back, urging her to continue walking. All the physical contact from him was making her head spin.

When they entered their room, Alethia spun to face Odeza and crossed her arms. "May I speak now?" She sassed.

Odeza's mouth quirked at the corners and amusement flickered in his eyes briefly before it was gone.

"You may."

"Are you going to tell me what the hell is going on?"

"Yes. I needed us to speak in private . . . with complete privacy. Which is why our phones needed to stay in the car."

Alethia furrowed her brow. "Are you telling me my phone is tapped?"

"I don't know that for sure. I just wanted to be cautious. Come here, please." He motioned for her to sit beside him on the bed.

She obeyed him.

"I'm not trying to freak you out. I just want to be transparent with you about some things because I need you to know I ... well, I care about you," he began clumsily. Alethia had never seen Odeza so unsure of himself. "You kept asking me why you were on this trip and what the purpose was. The reasons I gave you were true, but there is a little more to it." He held her piercing gaze. "You've been standing out among the others who were hired along with you. Anytime Ascensio employees begin to shine in whatever area they are in, leadership is keen to recruit those employees to our Special Interests Division. It was important for you to see our different facilities to learn about the *advances* we're making in our labs with the treatment you saw at SeaPoint—and the *great need* for those advances, as you saw in Allsbrook and here in Fort Kenzington today. Like I told you before, the information about the serum is not information just anyone gets to know." Odeza paused, letting what he was telling her sink in.

"Okay . . . " Alethia thought through what Odeza was saying. "So far this sounds like . . . not a bad thing?" Alethia questioned. What was the need for secrecy?

Odeza glided his tongue over his bottom lip and bit it. His face looked pained, like he was battling internally with something.

"It's *not* a bad thing," he assured. "But what I need you to know about the purpose of this trip—and what I'm not *supposed* to tell you—is that you are meant to prove yourself to me, and therefore Ascensio, so they can judge whether to bring you on to the Division."

Alethia raised an eyebrow and stared, waiting for him to continue. She didn't like the sound of that one bit.

"One of the core dedications of this division is recruitment of people who are suffering to receive services. There are a lot of people in this world, as you know, that desperately need a reprieve from their suffering. And I know you *also* know that not everyone knows how to get it.

"Ascensio needs to know if you value their mission and can carry out its goals. But I want y*ou* to decide that for yourself. I don't want this to be their decision—I want it to be y*ours*, if you want it. I want you to tell me what you want," Odeza finished. He pressed his fingertips together and eyed her, clearly nervous about her response.

Alethia's mind swirled. She felt enraged that she was being put through a test without her knowledge to ultimately be judged. At the same time, she was also inspired by the drive to help suffering people get the help they needed. Odeza was absolutely correct that the suffering she'd seen at the Allsbrook facility and Fort Kenzington facility alone was enough to prove the value of a potential cure.

If Ascensio's labs were on the brink of a complete game-changer for the field of mental health, it would be a dream come true to bear witness to lives being changed like that.

If what happened for the patients at SeaPoint could happen for everyone else . . . if it was legitimate, and *safe* . . . how could she not stand behind a movement like that? Part of her understood why the information needed to be kept confidential. They were patients with the right to privacy, after all, and the serum was still being tested. She was intrigued and felt compelled to know all there was to know about it.

The fact that Odeza wanted her to make her own choice and was putting himself at risk by telling her all of this filled her with warmth. There was a tugging sensation in her chest that made her want to reach for him. His eyes were molten steel with a glimmering black pool at the center where his pupils seemed to be dilated slightly. He was so beautiful.

"Say something, please," he beseeched her in a whisper. "What do you want?"

What did she *want*?

The sound of him begging completely undid her.

Alethia closed the gap between them in one swift maneuver and pulled him down to press her lips to his. She felt Odeza's body stiffen briefly in surprise before grabbing her hips as she swung her leg around to straddle his lap.

What was she doing? Why did this man unravel every ounce of self-control she possessed? Why did she crave him so intensely?

She ran her fingers through his hair and held him by the back of the neck, pressing her mouth harder onto his. He let out a soft groan and ran his hands up her thighs, causing her to arch her back. Shoving him back so he was flat on the bed, she continued to kiss him thoroughly. Odeza's breath caught at the action. She began unbuttoning his shirt, desperate to feel his skin. Needing to see his gorgeous torso and run her hands along his toned abdomen. When she got his shirt undone, she did just that.

Without warning, Odeza easily rolled them, pinning her to the bed. Panting, he hovered over her, gazing into her eyes with a ravenous look on his face.

"You don't want to do that," Odeza growled.

"Yes, I do," she challenged him.

"Alethia," Odeza protested between heavy breaths.

"Why not?" she demanded.

"You *know* why not."

She raised an eyebrow. "You want me to stop?"

He sighed deeply. "You know the answer to that, too."

"Then what's wrong?"

"What's wrong is that we're almost at the point of no return—and I can't let you waste yourself on me," he ground out.

"You aren't seriously going to play the '*you're too good for me*' card, are you?"

Odeza leveled a stare at her.

"All I'm saying is you should let me decide that for myself," she amended, and began tracing a line with her pointer finger where his pants met his waist. Odeza inhaled sharply. He took her hand and pinned it up by her head, then leaned down, nearly grazing their noses together.

"*Alethia.*"

She tilted her head and brought it up so their lips were a fraction of an inch apart. "Fine, then . . . if you want me to stop, *get off of me*," she breathed.

29. JAXON
DECEMBER 2072

Jaxon stared up at the giant glass infrastructure resembling an egg in a nest that was Ascensio, Inc. He had just driven six hours through the night from Fort Kenzington. Mora's parents had called to tell him that his girlfriend had been checked into a mental institution. He ran a hand over his face and downed the last of his gas station coffee. The clock in his Jeep read 7:45. Visiting hours started at 8.

He blew a long exhale out of his lips and willed himself to get out of the car. The lady at the security gate told him to follow the signs for the main entrance. The instructions were simple, but the task was not.

This place is a damn maze, Jaxon cursed.

By the time he found the correct entrance and made his way through the lobby, it was 8:15. He approached the receptionist.

"Good morning, sir, how can I help you?" She beamed, speaking with a voice that was *way* too shrill for the early hour.

"I'm here to visit Mora D'Angelo," he rasped and cleared his throat.

"Your relation, sir?"

"I'm her boyfriend."

"I see." She clicked away at her keyboard. "Please sign in here and fill out your visitor's name tag," she said, still smiling like an idiot.

Jaxon was not in the mood for pleasantries.

"And I will need you to leave any cell phone or electronic device here with me," she chirped. "I'll take good care of it until you're ready to leave!"

"Why do you need my phone?" Jaxon demanded.

"It is a policy we have here to protect the privacy of our patients. We do not allow photos to be taken or any electronic device that is capable of such to enter the facility." Her voice and facial features, although just as sugar-coated as before, adopted an underlying sternness that conveyed there was no further discussion on the matter.

Jaxon sighed and handed over his phone.

Upon his compliance, the receptionist lifted her features once more to their plastered pleasantness. She escorted him down a hallway and into a private room.

"I will inform Mora's caretakers you are here; we will do what we can to make your wait as short as possible," she said, and left him.

Jaxon fidgeted in his chair. He had never heard of Ascensio, Incorporated. He felt a heaviness in him that he couldn't push completely away.

He felt guilty.

He had thought she was doing so much better before he left for Fort Kenzington. He never would have left her alone if he'd known this would happen. The last few years had been so hard on their relationship. He felt guilty for being exhausted by it. A helplessness had grown within him, coupled by frustration by the lack of any idea how to help her.

Alone with his thoughts, Jaxon took in his surroundings. Several padded chairs that looked comfortable, but were in fact *not*, encircled a round table. The walls, painted a nondescript beige, were adorned with a handful of cheap, generic flower paintings. A lone tissue box occupied the center of the table, the room's sole concession to comfort. Otherwise, the room was starkly unadorned—apart from a camera in the corner, its lens fixed on him, a red light blinking steadily.

So, this private room was not so private after all. Jaxon hated that Mora was here. But her parents had told him that it had been her decision. Apparently, she had been seeing a psychiatrist here and decided to check herself in.

Jaxon drummed his fingers on the table. Without his phone, he had no idea what time it was, but he estimated he had probably been sitting there for thirty minutes.

At last, the door clicked open. He straightened in his chair and perked up as a woman in pink scrubs and a low ponytail appeared. She smiled at Jaxon, holding the door open behind her.

Mora, dressed in a plain, long-sleeved white gown, timidly entered the room. Jaxon noted the dark circles under her eyes. She looked thin. Her hair was stringy, and she almost seemed . . . *confused.*

"Mora's feeling a little groggy this morning," the woman in scrubs said. "She started a new medication recently that tends to leave patients a little lethargic for the first few days as they adjust to it."

Mora took a seat in one of the chairs and looked blankly at Jaxon. Like she didn't recognize him.

"Medication for what, exactly?" Jaxon fired at the woman.

"Sir, while Mora has designated you as an emergency contact with visitation rights, she hasn't granted you access to her medical information. I'm not at liberty to discuss that with you," the woman replied, her tone respectful yet firm. She turned to Mora and placed a hand on her shoulder. "You, however, can talk to him about your treatment, and anything else you like—okay, Sweetie? I'll leave you two to visit." She promptly left the room.

As the door shut behind her, Jaxon sat back in his chair and looked to Mora. She was now staring at the table.

"Mora?" Jaxon said softly.

She looked up at him with a quizzical look on her face.

"Mora, do you know who I am?" Jaxon questioned as gently as possible.

"Of course, I know who you *are*," she croaked from her dry lips then narrowed her eyes. "You, *Jaxon*, are the boyfriend who abandoned me," she scoffed.

"Mora . . . I . . . I didn't abandon you. I . . . *Shit*. I'm sorry, babe. I'm so sorry I left while you were . . . struggling." Tears stung as they welled in Jaxon's eyes. "I hate seeing you in this place . . . like this."

"Well, I like it here. I'm doing just fine."

"You don't *look* fine."

"Oh, really? Still not good enough for you, huh? Why did you even come here if all you're going to do is criticize me? I came here to get *help*, Jaxon. To try to *fix* myself, like you were always so keen to make me realize I needed to." Mora sat back in her seat and crossed her arms, turning away from him with a scowl.

Her words dug into him like a fire poker that had been sitting in coals. It had never been his intention to make her feel that way. He blinked back the tears that were threatening to fall.

"I never meant to do that, Mora," he whispered. "I'm sorry."

"You know what, I'm glad you came today," she said and looked back at him. He noticed her pupils were dilated unnaturally and she was slurring her words slightly. "I don't think we should see each other anymore. At least not while I'm in here trying to get better."

Jaxon studied her. She seemed to be a completely different woman from when he last saw her. Worry and fear pricked at his spine. Something seemed so incredibly off with her.

"Are you sure everything is okay in here?" Jaxon asked, becoming more and more alarmed.

She shook her head and let out an exasperated huff. "I just broke up with you and you didn't even acknowledge it."

"I'm really worried about you, Mora. What is the medication they have you on?" he pressed.

"It's none of your damn business," she retorted, "I want you to leave."

"Mora . . . "

"*I want you to leave.*"

As if on cue, the door opened and the woman in pink scrubs informed Jaxon it was time for him to go.

30. ALETHIA
FEBRUARY 2073

Alethia stared at the clock in the bottom corner of her computer screen. 4:47 pm. She stifled a yawn. It had been a long day.

In fact, since she'd returned from her trip with Odeza, every day had been a long day. It had been exhausting getting back into the swing of things at work. Even though some of her teammates had been assigned to help take on her caseload of intakes, she had returned to a giant box of files on her desk that she needed to enter into the computer before storing in the file room.

She debated staying late to try to get caught up. If so, she was going to need more caffeine. Alethia grabbed her coffee mug off her desk and headed to one of the employee lounges.

DISSIPATION

She poured some coffee into the mug and began looking in the cabinets for sugar. Of course, it was up on one of the higher shelves. She sighed and stood on the tips of her toes to try to reach it.

"Need a hand?"

A voice she knew so well sent a shiver down her spine. She slowly turned and found Odeza leaning on the door frame with a smug look of amusement from watching her try—and fail—to reach the sugar.

"I assume *you're* the one who put it all the way up there," she replied, crossing her arms. "You should try thinking about somebody other than yourself for a change. Not all of us are six feet tall around here."

"You know, you're right," he said, sauntering across the room. He stopped within inches of her. She was suddenly overcome by the sensations of his cologne and body heat. Her stomach squirmed. "The least I could do is set it down lower for the vertically challenged."

The words dripped from his lips like honey. He held her gaze as he looked down at her, never breaking eye contact, as he reached up to grab the sugar. Leaning even closer, he set it on a lower shelf.

"Really?" She mused, shooting him a look of feigned annoyance. "You're not even going to get it all the way down for me?"

He placed his hands on the counter on either side of her. "Now why would I do that? I know how much you like to take matters into your own hands."

Alethia felt heat rising to her cheeks as she recalled their encounter in the hotel room. Her chest rose and fell as she attempted to regulate her breathing. Cocking her head to the side, she took the bait. She turned around to face the counter, his arms still enclosing her on either side.

The sugar was still ever so slightly out of her reach. She licked her lips and pressed them together.

"Ah, still out of reach? My mistake," he whispered in her ear. One of his hands grazed her hip and lower back while the other ran along her still-outstretched arm on its way up to the sugar. He set down the jar, his fingers trailing her sides again, then dipped the spoon into the sugar jar and scooped it into her mug. Alethia remained incredibly still. Her heart raced and her cheeks burned.

What was this man doing to her?

"Do you want more?" he breathed into her ear.

Alethia took the mug and turned back around to face him. His eyes met hers with greedy intent. A smile played at the corners of his mouth. He was enjoying himself way too much.

With her free hand, Alethia ran her hand up his chest a few inches before stopping and pushed into his upper pectoral, savoring that firmness and warmth.

Her push was enough to make him step back. He raised his eyebrows at her.

"That's plenty," she replied, tossing him a semi-sweet smile and grazing past him as she strode out of the room.

31. JAXON
FEBRUARY 2073

It had been two months since Jaxon had visited Mora in Ascensio. He had tried to get back into his daily routines and respect what she had told him—that they were over.

But he couldn't stop thinking about her.

About how angry she'd been with him.

How sick she'd looked.

How wrong the whole thing had seemed.

Jaxon knew he needed to see her again, even if it was just to end things on a better note. He didn't want them to be over, but he understood she needed to focus on herself.

He needed to see her, just one more time, to gain some kind of closure on the situation... and to make sure she was truly okay.

DISSIPATION

Jaxon got up very early on a Saturday and once again made the six-hour drive back to see Mora. He made it to Ascensio by 10:00 AM. He had called the visitors center the day before to inform them of his intent to visit, just to make sure she hadn't told them she no longer wanted him to have that access.

Luckily, she had not removed him from the visitor's list.

Jaxon found himself sitting in the exact same chair in the exact same room he had sat in two months ago when he'd seen Mora last. The door clicked open just as it had that morning, but this time, Mora pushed it open herself and walked into the room with an energetic cadence.

She was like an early summer breeze. Vibrant, fresh, and full of new life. Her cheeks were rosy. Her soft brown hair was brushed and parted evenly down the middle. She was still in a plain white gown, but she had put on weight, looking healthy once more.

"Hello, Jaxon," she said as she sat down and smiled at him.

"Mora . . . Hi . . . you look *amazing*," he stated the obvious.

Mora tucked her hair behind her ear and folded her hands in front of her, "Why thank you. To what do I owe the pleasure of your visit?"

Okay . . . this was odd. Mora was behaving as if they were old friends with no baggage between them. As if they hadn't dated for years and broken up only two months ago after she'd reached an all-time low with her mental health.

"Well, I just, um. I just felt like things ended badly last time. I've thought about you every day, Mora. I miss you. And I love you, I always will, you know that. I guess I just had to see you again to make sure things were okay here and that . . . you were okay."

Mora blinked. "Of course, I'm okay. I'm better than ever," was her only reply.

"That's great," Jaxon began. He felt slightly hurt by her curt reply to his heartfelt speech. "So, does that mean you get to go home now?"

Mora blinked again and furrowed her eyebrows.

"Home?" she repeated in a confused tone. "This *is* my home, now. I decided to join Ascensio's permanent residence program." Mora beamed and gushed, "I've never felt so alive and wonderful. Ascensio has changed my life, and I couldn't imagine leaving this place."

Never leave this place? Panic began rising in Jaxon's chest.

"You can't be serious, Mora. You can't stay here *forever*!" he exclaimed.

She smiled condescendingly at him, as though she were talking to a child. "You know better than anyone that my life was a mess before I came here. I had nothing to live for. Why would I leave? There would be nothing to go back to," she stated candidly, as a matter of fact with no feeling.

Ouch. *He* was part of that 'nothing to go back to'.

Jaxon felt like this was a complete stranger sitting across the table. This was not the Mora he knew. The way she spoke, the way she carried herself, the things she said, they were all unrecognizable.

"Well, I should probably be getting back," Mora said cheerily after a few minutes of silence. *Back to what?* She stood and made her way to the door before he could respond. Just before exiting, Mora turned back and looked him square in the eyes. With a plastered smile, she said, "It was nice to see you, Jason."

With that, she was gone.

Jaxon blinked. His girlfriend of five years and the love of his life had just called him *Jason*.

32. JAXON
FEBRUARY 2073

"What the hell did you people do to my girlfriend?" Jaxon demanded of the receptionist back in the lobby. "She seemed like she couldn't care less who I was. She called me by the *wrong name!*" he seethed.

"Sir, I need you to calm down," the receptionist intoned, motioning with her hands for him to lower his voice as if he was a child throwing a tantrum.

"I want to talk to her doctor. Something's not right here," Jaxon raged. "My girlfriend of five years doesn't know my *name*?" Like hell he was going to calm down.

"Dr. Pine is extremely busy, I'm afraid. That won't be possible," she replied, then resumed typing on her computer as if he were no longer in front of her.

"I don't think you understand. I'm not leaving until I get some answers," Jaxon drawled out the last sentence slowly to emphasize his point.

"Sir, there is nothing I can do for you. Mora has responded to treatment exceptionally well, and it would be a hindrance to her were I to allow you to stay here and carry on like this." The woman looked at Jaxon like he was an annoying fly buzzing in her ear. "*So*, you can either exit on your own volition, or I can have security *remove* you."

Out of the corner of his eye, Jaxon saw something fall to the floor. A blonde employee walking through the lobby had dropped a box of files and was muttering curses as she haphazardly gathered them. Seemingly aware she was being watched, she looked up and locked eyes with him.

Jaxon's jaw dropped as he stared. He'd seen this woman before, in the bar at Fort Kenzington after he had just returned from his first visit with Mora. She'd asked him if he was okay, and he'd told her he'd just been dumped. What were the odds of seeing her in that bar and her being an employee in the facility where his girlfriend had forgotten his name? However, she appeared just as shocked to see him.

"*You*," he said, taking a step towards her. He was stopped by two large men each taking hold of one of his arms.

"It's time for you to go, sir," one of them groused in a deep voice.

Jaxon's fight-or-flight response kicked in, and Jaxon ran through his options in his head. He could try to break from the clutches of these men, which was highly unlikely, or he could do as they said and wait to figure out his next move until later, outside of this place. He opted for the latter.

"Fine," he acquiesced.

The men led him through the doors and watched him until he got into his car.

Inside the car, Jaxon breathed heavily. His heart raced. What the hell was going on? And what the *hell* was he going to do about it? He started his car. He would have to come up with some kind of plan. He needed to call Mora's parents.

Suddenly, there was a tap on his passenger window. Startled, he turned to find the blonde woman from Fort

Kenzington motioning for him to roll his window down. He quickly did.

She handed him a business card that read, "*Alethia Burkshire, Ascensio, Inc. Intake Specialist*," followed by a phone number. He looked on the back. In scribbled ink it read: *Meet me at Haven's Coffee House on Fillmore Street at six o'clock tonight.*

When he looked back up, she was gone.

33. MORA
FEBRUARY 2073

Mora was startled by a soft knock on the door to her room. She had been resting on her bed, struggling to overcome the slight headache and uneasy feeling that had followed the conversation with her visitor earlier that morning.

"It's time for your treatment, Sweetie," Mora's caretaker, Stephanie, called from the other side of the door.

"Coming," Mora called back. She pulled herself out of bed and put her shoes and a sweater on. It was always chilly in the treatment room.

"How are you today?" Stephanie asked in her usual happy-go-lucky tone as they walked the bright white halls.

"I'm great," Mora blurted without much thought.

Inside the treatment room, Mora sat in her usual pale blue, leather cushioned chair that faced a large TV screen and put her headset on. The probes no longer hurt like they had when she first began the treatments. These days, she felt little more than a slight tingle. Placing the earbuds in her ears, she rolled up her sleeve so she could receive her medicine.

Stephanie injected Mora with the clear liquid and turned on the large TV. Within moments, Mora felt the serum traveling through her veins like droplets from an icicle traveling down the frozen shaft before falling to the ground. The quiet numbness of her consciousness that she'd grown accustomed to began to take its effect. She turned her attention to the TV.

On the screen, a scene of her graduating high school and earning honors played before her. She listened to the voice coming from the headset. *Your high school graduation*, it said.

"My high school graduation," Mora repeated.

The scene changed, and she watched herself waving goodbye to her parents. *Your parents are so proud of you to be getting the help you need at Ascensio*, the voice commented.

"My parents are proud of me for being here," she parroted.

The scene changed to the living quarters of Ascensio, and she saw herself laughing and smiling with the other residents. *You love being here and you don't want to leave*, the voice told her.

"I love being here and I don't want to leave."

Next, she saw herself with the same man that visited her today. He was yelling at her, and she ran from him. *You don't want to see this man again. You don't remember his significance in your life.*

"I don't want to see that man again and I don't remember his significance in my life."

84. ALETHIA
FEBRUARY 2073

The second the clock had struck 5:00 PM, Alethia nearly sprinted out of her cubicle. She made a mad dash for her car in the parking garage. Her heart rate had been spiked for the entire afternoon and she hadn't been able to focus on a damn thing.

The man from the bar in Fort Kenzington had been irate in the visitor's lobby today when she'd been taking her box of files to the file room. She had a gut instinct that the two incidents could not be a coincidence. Something was going on, and she was determined to find out.

Alethia drove manically on the highway towards Fillmore Street where she'd told the man to meet her at Haven's Coffee House. Was it a good decision? To meet this stranger alone—a man who had seemed ready to pounce on the receptionist? Alethia pushed away the voice in her head that was telling her to slow down and take all aspects of the situation into careful consideration. She didn't have time for that.

Alethia parked on the street outside the coffee house. Despite being fifteen minutes early, she could see the man waiting for her already in a back corner booth. Alethia drew in a deep breath and blew it out slowly through her lips. *Here we go.*

A tiny bell dinged as she opened the door, and the man's brown eyes locked onto hers immediately. His shaggy brown hair was unkempt, and he looked like he hadn't slept in days. Five O'clock shadow speckled his chin. His leg bounced erratically under the table.

Alethia took another deep breath as she approached the man. She sat in front of him at the booth. Neither of them said anything until a waitress asked for her order.

"I'll just have black coffee, thank you," Alethia said quietly. The waitress nodded and filled a mug, then walked away. Alethia looked back to the man.

"Hi," she offered cautiously. "I'm Alethia."

"Jaxon," he replied shortly.

"I saw you at a bar in Fort Kenzington," Alethia stated the obvious, not sure how they were to begin this conversation or where it would take them.

He nodded, "And I saw you."

"Right. You looked very upset earlier today. What was that about?" She queried.

His eyes narrowed. "You expect me to believe you have no knowledge of what was going on? You work there, don't you?" The man's tone remained hushed, but each word struck her like a viper.

She raised her hands in a gesture of innocence. "Look, the whole reason I'm here is to try to understand what's going on—and to see if I can help. Okay? I *truly* don't know what's going on."

He studied her for a moment, setting his jaw. Upon his appraisal, he must have judged her as telling the truth.

He replied, "I visited my girlfriend Mora—well, ex-girlfriend, I guess—of five years, and she acted like a robot. She didn't even know my name."

Mora. Alethia recognized that name. She had done Mora's intake back in December. She furrowed her brow.

"I met her," Alethia admitted. "I actually did her intake."

Jaxon raised an eyebrow at her.

"Well," he said quietly, the leash on his anger slipping, "Something's wrong with her. I know she had problems she was working on, but the woman I saw today was a completely different person. She told me, the last time I saw her, that they were giving her some kind of new medication. She looked pretty rough during that visit. Today, however, she looked like all her problems had been solved, and she didn't give a shit about me. She didn't seem to know who I was." Jaxon was balling up a napkin in his fist.

A notion clicked into place for Alethia. *A new medication.* Could this be the serum? But if she didn't seem to know an intimate partner of five years...

This was bad. So bad. She needed to talk to Odeza. He needed to give her answers. Alethia felt anger building in her chest. If he knew more about this serum than he had told her...

"Listen," Alethia implored. "I just started working at Ascensio, and I'm going to be honest with you. I have had a weird feeling about some of the methods they've put into practice. I'm going to find Mora and talk to her, ok? I'm going to do everything I can to help her. To help you."

The sincerity in her voice softened Jaxon's scowl ever so slightly. He sat back in his seat, his lips in a firm line. He looked into her eyes, seeming to search for any reason not to trust her.

"Okay. I appreciate your help. Please let me know what you find out," he replied.

On Alethia's way back out to her car, she slid her phone out of her pocket and fired Odeza a text that read: *Meet me at my apartment ASAP.*

35. ALETHIA
FEBRUARY 2073

Alethia sat on her couch facing her flat's front door. She tapped her foot impatiently. Thankfully, Odeza had said he was on his way as soon as she'd demanded he come over.

There was a knock at the door.

Alethia jumped up to answer it.

"Missed me already?" he teased her. She had no time for his flirtations. She pulled him by the arm through the door, kicking it closed.

"Whoa, easy," he said as she pushed him down on the couch. "What is—"

"I need you to stop talking and listen, Odeza. This is extremely serious, and I need you to tell me the truth," she demanded, fixing him with an intense, unwavering gaze.

Odeza's amused cadence immediately fell, and he blinked at her. "What's going on?"

"Does Ascensio's elusive miracle serum have memory-erasing side effects?" Alethia directly asked, not bothering to beat around the bush.

"That's ridiculous, Alethia. Of course not."

"Are you *sure*?"

Odeza paused and furrowed his brow.

"I don't know much about how it works, truthfully . . . but why would you think it erases people's memories? That seems like it would be counterproductive to one's treatment," he retorted.

Alethia crossed her arms and began to pace.

"Why was the boyfriend of one of our Desert View patients in the Fort Kenzington bar we went to?" Alethia questioned.

"What? When did you even—how am *I* supposed to know? Do you think I keep track of every one of our patients' relatives?"

"So, you don't know who Jaxon is?"

"No?" Odeza was looking at her like she was insane.

"Things are not making sense, Odeza! And you're looking at me like I've gone crazy, but I'm telling you the truth. This Jaxon guy just so happened to be at the bar we were at. Then I saw him in the lobby today, and he was freaking out. So, I met him at a coffee shop just now, and he—"

"You did *what?*" Odeza interjected, springing to his feet and hurrying towards her.

Alethia ignored his interruption. She continued pacing as she rattled off what had happened, perhaps more for her own understanding of the incidents at this point.

" . . . and he told me that he met with his ex-girlfriend Mora today and she was completely healthy and happy looking, yet she didn't seem to remember him—"

"Alethia, you met with some strange guy who was throwing a fit in the lobby? A visitor of one of our *patients?*" Odeza was in front of her now.

"She had called him by the wrong name, and they had been dating for years. And she told him she'd taken this new *medication—*"

"Alethia, *stop.* Stop for a second," Odeza pleaded. He took her wrists gently to stop her from continuing to pace past him. He walked her backwards until her back was against the nearby wall. His eyes brimmed with concern as he searched her face.

"*What*? Are you listening to how crazy this is?" Alethia sputtered.

"Oh, I hear some crazy," he huffed, exasperated.

"Screw you," Alethia snapped. She tried pulling away, but his grip tightened. He brought his body closer to hers as he held her hands up against his chest.

"*Wait*. Wait. I'm sorry. I don't think you're crazy. I need you to slow down. Can we back up to the 'meeting a strange man at a coffee shop' part, please?" Odeza coaxed.

Alethia let out a sigh. She cursed herself for it, but she was so aware of Odeza's proximity and every part of him that was in contact with her. Electricity seemed to pulse between them as they looked into each other's eyes.

"When I recognized him in the lobby and saw how upset he was, I followed him out to his car and gave him my card with directions to meet me at Haven's Coffee House tonight so I could figure out what was going on," Alethia clarified, speaking slower. "Basically, his ex-girlfriend is one of our patients, a patient whose intake I did, and she's turned into an unrecognizable version of herself who doesn't seem to know who her boyfriend of five years is after taking a *new medication.*"

Odeza frowned down at her in thought. "So, you're wondering if it's the new serum that's causing her memory problems," Odeza finished her thought.

"*Yes,*" Alethia affirmed.

Odeza let go of her and stepped away. He appeared deep in thought, processing what she'd said. He sat down on the couch and let out a heavy sigh, running a hand over his face.

"*So*? Do you know anything about this I don't? Is it possible?" Alethia pressed.

"I don't know," Odeza admitted, a weary expression on his face.

Alethia came to sit down next to him. "What *do* you know about the serum?"

Odeza eyed her. He sighed again, and appeared to debate saying what crossed his mind.

"I think, first, it's important for you to know the history of Ascensio," he began and sat back into the couch, crossing one leg over a knee, spreading his hands out over his leg. "Ascensio, Incorporated was founded in 2050 just after the second Dark Age, as I'm sure you know. Society in the 2040s was bleak. Suicide rates had skyrocketed, and mental health issues of all kinds were so prevalent because of the collapse of the government, poverty rates, all of that.

"Ascensio started out as a lab created to research and develop new psychotropic medication since the ones that existed were becoming useless. The government funded the lab because it believed it could help get people back on their feet as society was rebuilding itself.

"In 2055, a neuroscientist by the name of Analysa Khordsmith discovered the brain sequences for SI and depression. Medication was created to try and destroy the neural sequences of depression and SI, but even as they killed off some, the body seemed to regenerate more. Even after years of frustration, Analysa was not able to cure all the patients, so she started experimenting with memory. She theorized that if the patients couldn't remember what was causing them distress, even subconsciously, then perhaps that would cure them of their depression and people would no longer want to take their own life.

"Analysa began experimenting on several patients—*willing* patients, mind you—by destroying certain neural sequences in their hippocampus. However, it was impossible for Analysa to determine which memories were linked to the depression, and it left her patients with gaps in their memory that only made their conditions worse.

"So, the government pulled its funding to focus on other areas of society that were in desperate need. Analysa's lab was shut down and Ascensio began to venture down the path of rehabilitative and residential care—which remains its focus to this day.

"The serum they've been working on is still so new that they're probably still working the kinks out. My role doesn't involve the lab, so I'm not privy to the information you want—about how it works and what its contraindications are . . . I just, I can't imagine they are intentionally screwing with people's memory, Alethia, but I just don't know . . . " Odeza finished with a frown as if considering the possibility that she had insinuated.

Alethia was at a loss for words. From what he'd just told her it sounded way more plausible than she had originally thought that they were manipulating Mora's memory. Not just Mora's—probably *every* patient who was trialing the serum. A knot was growing bigger and bigger in Alethia's stomach, and she thought she might be sick.

"I need to talk to Mora," Alethia decided aloud.

Odeza looked at her. He was chewing on his inner cheek in thought. His eyes held a look of fear.

"There's another thing you need to know, Alethia. Ascensio is very strict about its policies. Confidentiality, protocols, all of that. If you start digging around too much, they're going to notice and . . . " He trailed off, running his hands through his hair and then rubbing his closed eyelids with his thumb and index finger. *Was he scared?* Odeza's anxiety was palpable.

"And *what*?" Alethia pressed.

"And I need you to promise me you won't do anything that will put you at odds with those *policies*. Bad things happen to those who break the rules, and I can't let anything bad happen to you."

"What bad things?" Alethia asked slowly, her brows drawing further together.

"It doesn't matter. Because you aren't going to do anything stupid," Odeza implored.

"Is it 'stupid' to try to understand if someone is okay? That they aren't at the mercy of a science experiment? I wouldn't call that stupid, Odeza, I'd call that *humane*," Alethia asserted, raising her voice slightly.

Odeza pressed his lips together and shook his head. "You're going to need my help."

"That's more like it."

36. ALETHIA
FEBRUARY 2073

Alethia's heart raced. She pulled at the cuffs of her sweater and tapped her foot to the beat of a hummingbird's wings. She and Odeza had spent hours the night before going over a plan that they believed would not draw attention as she attempted to meet with Mora. Alethia would wait in her cubicle until Odeza gave her the signal it was time to move. She stared at her computer screen but saw nothing as her mind rehearsed their plan.

Then, out of the corner of her eye, she saw Odeza enter the staff lounge. That was her cue. She grabbed her coffee mug and forced herself to go to the lounge slowly and casually.

Odeza was waiting in there for her. He leaned against the counter with a mug in his hand and a relaxed posture that portrayed he hadn't a care in the world. His eyes, however, doused her in hot water. They sang to her. There was so much communication in that one look. He was telling her to be careful. And, perhaps, that he had faith in her too.

"Coffee?" he asked her for the sake of the camera that was in the corner of the room.

"Thanks," she replied cordially and walked up to him.

"Allow me," he said, turning his body towards her, his broad shoulders and towering physique momentarily blocking the camera's view as he grabbed the coffee pot. With one skillful maneuver he placed one of his hands over the top of hers briefly, sliding his keycard into her sweater sleeve as he poured the coffee into her mug with the other hand.

Before backing away, his lips brushed her forehead and he muttered, "Please be careful."

She savored his heat, his smell, the reassurance of his body being so close to hers, the tingling sensation his fingers left behind on her hand.

"Thanks for the coffee," she said, taking her mug and exiting the room.

She returned to her cubicle and marked the time. 10:07. Odeza had instructed her to give him five minutes to find Patrick and distract him before she made her move to leave the office area. Patrick always seemed to have his eyes on her, though for a reason she satisfyingly knew drove Odeza insane.

After a few minutes, she heard Odeza say in a loud, sarcastic tone, "Patty, how *are* you, old friend?"

It was now or never. Alethia pushed her chair back from her desk and stood. She smoothed out her skirt and headed for the hallway that would take her towards the residential facility. With each footstep that echoed down the cold and sterile linoleum hallway, her heart pounded.

Odeza never did say what would happen to Alethia if she was caught, but he'd seemed up in arms about it last night. But it couldn't be *that* bad, right? The worst they could do was fire her. Right?

She continued walking. She could see the employee restroom ahead, which Odeza told her to look out for. He'd told her he was going to ask one of the new hires to leave an extra pair of residential caretaker scrubs in the end stall for an employee that had soiled scrubs from a resident throwing up on them and was trying to be discreet about it. To her annoyance, Odeza had assured Alethia that the employee he'd asked to do this task for him had googly eyes for him and would do whatever he asked without question because she wanted his approval.

To Alethia's great relief, the bathroom was empty when she entered. She took a breath before opening the end stall door. There they were: the pink scrubs. She blew the air out between her lips that she hadn't realized she'd been holding and willed herself to calm down. Her fluttering heart disobeyed her.

Alethia never broke the rules. She never blatantly disobeyed authority. What she was about to do did both of those things. Yet, Alethia held tightly to her conviction that something was not right, and she was determined to get answers to help someone who was potentially being victimized for the sake of research.

Alethia quickly changed into the scrubs and put her hair into a low ponytail as Odeza had instructed. There was also a paper facemask and disposable gloves with the scrubs that Odeza had told the employee to leave with the changes of clothes *in case the patient had spread germs to the employee who got thrown up on.* Alethia had to admit, Odeza had thought of everything.

She took one more deep breath before stashing her clothes in an airtight, waterproof bag that she had folded up tightly and put in her bra that morning. She placed the bag of her clothing in the refill water basin at the back of the toilet and placed the lid carefully back in place. Not the most ideal part of their plan, but she had no other options if they didn't want any suspicions being drawn.

Last night, Alethia had printed a photo of herself with the description "Ascensio Residential Caretaker" that she slid into the case of Odeza's badge over his photo. This way, his fob, which had nearly unlimited access, could get her anywhere she wanted to go, but if she was stopped, her badge would match her description.

She recalled what Odeza had said to her. *Act like you're where you're supposed to be. Confidently move about and don't look like you don't know where you're going, even if you don't. The surer of yourself you look, the least likely it is someone will find you to be suspicious.*

Minding his advice, Alethia threw her shoulders back and raised her head high as she walked out of the bathroom and approached the wide metal double doors beholding a sign that, in red letters, said: *Residential Wing, Security Clearance Level Ten ONLY.*

Holding her breath, Alethia raised Odeza's fob up to the security pad and smiled beneath her medical mask as she heard the lock click open. She didn't hesitate as she pushed the door open and walked through.

She blinked as bright, fluorescent light hit her in the face. Alethia was greeted by a massive circular space with dozens of doors spaced evenly along the concave room around her. The metal doors all had a small window and a slot underneath that window with patient ID numbers labeled. In the center of the vast space was a colossal glass elevator shaft. Where it led, she could only guess.

There were several other caretakers in pink scrubs moseying about busily. Some pushed carts of food. Others walked with patients in white cotton outfits to and from the glass elevator. Several more double doors leading to different wings and hallways were dotted between the various patient rooms.

Don't talk to anybody if you can help it. If you can become invisible in the mix, minding your own business, you are most likely to stay under the radar. The other caretakers will be the ones most likely to not recognize you if you stop to ask questions. You need to have Mora's patient number memorized. Alethia recalled Odeza's words. She had pulled out Mora's intake form from December and located her patient number. 1407. Easy enough to remember.

Alethia willed herself forward amongst the shuffle and headed for the perimeter to find Mora's room number. She had to be fast. Every moment she was away from her cubicle was a moment for Patrick to realize she'd left. Every second she was where she wasn't supposed to be was another second she risked getting caught. So far, the plan had gone without a hitch, thanks to Odeza's planning and help—but it almost seemed *too* easy.

Patient 1407. Alethia had reached Mora's room. She prayed that Mora was in there. And that Mora was in there alone. Alethia peaked through the small window to find Mora sitting on her bed in a long white gown with her arms wrapped around her legs staring at the wall. Should she knock? She should probably knock, Alethia figured. She tapped softly on the door. Mora's eyes went to the window, and she made eye contact with Alethia but otherwise did not move or display any acknowledgement of her.

Alethia tapped Odeza's fob against the security pad outside of Mora's room and it clicked. She entered and shut the door behind her.

Mora's room was small. A twin-sized metal framed bed was tucked against the wall with a mattress and green bedspread neatly made upon which Mora sat. There was a half wall providing minimal privacy to a toilet and sink in the corner opposite the bed. The walls were concrete but painted in bright colors to give the illusion of a welcoming space. But it was not welcoming at all. It was a colorful jail cell.

"Hi, Mora," Alethia whispered, taking off her face mask so Mora could see her, and hopefully recognize her.

Mora had been watching her since she'd entered, but she'd yet to have any other reaction—which gave Alethia a bad feeling in her stomach.

"Hello," Mora responded as her eyes seemed to track Alethia's face. Noting the small smile she offered, Mora offered the same expression in return. As if mimicking her.

"Mora, my name is Alethia. I did your intake here a few months ago. Do you remember me?" Alethia said gently.

Mora tilted her head to the side. A look of confusion swept over her face and was gone in an instant. "I don't believe we've met," was her response.

"Mora, we *have* met. And I met with Jaxon, too. He really misses you and cares about you. We want to try to help you."

"Jaxon? I don't know a Jaxon, I'm afraid," Mora replied in an emotionless tone, "and I do not need any help at this time, thank you." She returned to looking at the wall.

Horror pelted Alethia. This woman was merely a human shell. All of her former mannerisms were gone, her intonations absent, everything that had made her herself, completely dissipated. What had they done to her?

"Mora," she pleaded, knowing she would soon have to get out of here or be caught. "What are they doing to you? Do you remember what they have—"

Alethia was silenced by the clicking of the lock as Mora's door swung open.

In the doorframe stood a woman in a grey pencil skirt and matching blazer. Red lipstick adorned her snarled smirk. The badge pinned to her lowcut blouse read *Elizabeth Straumen*.

"What do we have here?" Elizabeth crooned.

37. ODEZA
FEBRUARY 2073

Nerves festered in Odeza's stomach as he stared at the clock. 10:45. Alethia should be back by now. They had agreed she had fifteen minutes to get in, talk to Mora, and get back to her cubicle so that the preening imbecile Patrick wouldn't notice she was gone. She was going to text Odeza as soon as she was back. But it had been thirty-three minutes since she'd risen from her cubicle, and she hadn't texted.

Something had gone wrong, he just knew it. Bile rose to his throat, and he was certain he was going to spew his breakfast.

This was a stupid plan. They never should have tempted fate like this. Odeza had helped her carry it out only because he knew she would attempt it either way, and she was guaranteed to fail on her own—and damn him if he was going to sit idly by as she stubbornly ignored his advice to leave the situation alone.

His phone buzzed. His heart leapt out of his chest as he fumbled for it.

Come to my office. Now. It was Elizabeth.

Odeza's adrenaline shot through the roof as his eyes nearly popped out of his head. It was over. It was all over.

He scrambled from his office chair and half-walked, half-ran down the hall to Elizabeth's office, not caring about any of the bewildered side glances he got from the two other employees in the hall.

His hand flew to the handle before he stopped himself. It was a known rule at Ascensio that you do not enter Elizabeth Straumen's office without knocking. Part of him didn't give a shit. The other part of him was so conditioned he couldn't help himself but dodge any of the potential nuisances that set her off. He cursed himself as the latter instinct won and he rapped the door with his knuckles.

"Come in," she called out with a semi-sweet cadence of triumph in her voice. A piece of Odeza shriveled up and died as he opened the door.

No sooner did he enter than two of Elizabeth's specially assigned security guards had Odeza by the arms. His eyes darted to Elizabeth's.

Her eyes shone black and cold as she smirked, eyeing him up and down. She clacked her talon-like manicured nails on the glass surface of her desk.

"Do you want to tell me why our new little intake specialist, who you became *so* close to on your botched assignment, had access to your key card, Dezzy?" Her voice was an ice pick to his spine.

"Elizabeth—I can explain—" Odeza's voice cracked as he broke through the hysteria that threatened to overtake him.

"Oh, save it," she hissed. "You've been a very bad boy, darling, and you're going to have to be punished," she mocked with feigned sorrow.

Elizabeth grabbed a small remote that controlled the large TV monitor that hung from the wall adjacent to her desk. She clicked once and the monitor turned on.

Magnified terror locked Odeza in place as he saw a live security camera stream of Alethia, her hands and feet shackled to an exam room bed and a piece of duct tape on her mouth as she thrashed in the bed. Next to her, a doctor in a white lab coat was preparing a syringe with a clear serum.

"*No*," Odeza whimpered.

"Just thought you might like to say goodbye to your girlfriend," Elizabeth cackled as the doctor pushed the needle of the syringe into Alethia's arm.

38. ALETHIA
FEBRUARY 2073

Alethia sat in a pale blue, leather cushioned chair facing a large TV screen. There was a scene playing of her going into another patient's room. The girl she was talking to had long brown hair. A voice in her headset spoke to her, *"You don't know this woman and you don't remember anything about her."*

"I don't know that woman and I don't remember anything about her," Alethia repeated.

The scene changed to a video of her talking to a tall man with black hair and grey eyes. *You do not remember anything about Odeza Speer.*

"I don't remember anything about Odeza Speer."